VAUXHALL VICTOR
and the VX4/90

13-ISBN 978-1-84155-108-1

CONTENTS

Vauxhall Victor, Road Test	4
The Vauxhall Victor Estate Car	7
Vauxhall Victor Series 2 De Luxe	11
The Vauxhall Victor Super	15
Vauxhall VX Four-Ninety	19
Vauxhall Victor Estate Car	22
Brabham Converted Estate Car	26
Vauxhall Victor Estate Car	28
Vauxhall Victor 101 Estate Car	32
Vauxhall Victor 101 and VX4/90 Service Data	37
Vauxhall VX4/90 Road Test	53
Vauxhall VX4/90 Advert	59
Vauxhall VX4/90 Compare Your Car	60

Vauxhall Victor

DE LUXE SERIES 2

A trim strip extends the Vauxhall flute to give a continuous line from nose to tail, adding to the impression of length. Redesigned bumpers have increased strength and protect the corners of the body

IT is often by no means easy to modify an existing design entirely and still produce a pleasing, balanced appearance, but in the case of the new Series 2 Vauxhall Victors, described here and in *The Autocar*, 27 February, 1959, the change is decidedly for the better.

The overall impression created by the De Luxe model—the subject of this test—is that it is more tasteful and restrained than previous Victors. Inside the car, leather for seat covering, a more frugal use of colours and chromium, and a carpeted floor have given a marked air of quality to what is still a relatively low-priced car. A bench front seat would have only limited usefulness in a model which is intended to carry no more than four people, but three fairly slender adults were carried as an experiment for a short distance on the wide, close-spaced separate seats of this De Luxe version without discomfort.

Used normally, these seats are comfortable, giving good support to the thighs and shoulders, though the small-of-the-back support could be raised a little. Slight curving of the squabs gives some lateral location when cornering. With the seat adjusted fully back, a driver of average height and reach finds the pedals at the correct distance, but may think the wheel a little too close to the seat. For a long-legged driver, therefore, leg room is insufficient for comfort.

With a seat high in relation to the bottom of the windscreen and side windows, and to the steering wheel, a commanding driving position is achieved. Seat height and rake are adjustable by fitting or removing spacers beneath the seat mountings. The rigid, small-diameter wheel and fairly high-geared, accurate steering, give a fine sense of control. Good all-round visibility promotes confidence, particularly in heavy traffic, and as all four corners of the car are visible, placing, manoeuvring and reversing are made much easier.

A view of the road close to the front of the car is obtained over the low, flat bonnet. Visibility is good through the wrap-round screen but the wider angle of view is obtained only towards the bottom. The forward-sloping screen pillars are not wide, but become thicker towards the top in the line of sight most frequently used. Distortion at the ends was not troublesome. The rear-view mirror only occasionally forms a blind spot, and gives a good view through the wide rear window, though range is somewhat limited by the rear edge of the roof. Wing mirrors were excellent for keeping a check on overtaking or overtaken traffic.

Twin electric wipers clear the screen efficiently, and can be set at slow or fast speed according to conditions. However, they do leave a large unwiped area in the centre and at the curved ends, which limits visibility when the screen is spattered with mud. The wiper switch is pressed to operate the washers which are an optional extra.

Pedals are spaced well apart, and there is plenty of room to place the left foot comfortably beside the clutch. It would be an improvement if the brake pedal were more nearly at the level of the accelerator pedal, as the foot has to be lifted some distance to transfer it from accelerator to brake. It is necessary to reach well forward to apply the hand-brake, which is of the pull and twist type, and mounted immediately to the left of the steering column. It held the car securely on a one in three gradient without excessive effort. Twisting action is needed only when releasing the brake.

On the right of the facia is a combined ignition and starter switch. Removing the ignition key when the switch is in the vertical position locks the switch, but in one of the five positions, the key can be removed and the switch operated to turn on the ignition and start the engine. This enables the car to be started and driven in a service station while the owner retains the key. Starting was instantaneous from cold, the engine quickly reaching its normal running temperature.

A comfortable arc of movement is given by the clutch pedal, the clutch itself being smooth and light to operate. With one up and some test equipment aboard, a restart could just be made on a 1 in 4 gradient. A good example of a

Left: Above the new pancake-type intake filter is the two-speed windscreen wiper motor. Thermal interruptors are used instead of fuses in the electrical system of the Victor. Right: Torsion bars counterbalance the lid of the luggage boot, which has a very considerable depth for a car of this size. Tools and a scissors-type jack are carried behind the spare wheel

steering column gear change is fitted. It has short, positive movements between gears, and is almost free from lost motion. A praiseworthy feature of the Victor is the application of synchromesh to first in addition to the other two gears. It enables first gear to be engaged without special skill when on the move, and this is something which has to be done frequently in a car with a three-speed gear box. Synchromesh is effective provided that the changes are not hurried, and it was always possible to engage first gear without difficulty when at rest.

Performance, both in respect of actual figures, and the manner in which it was obtained, is an improvement on the earlier model. Acceleration from a standstill to 50 m.p.h., for example, takes three seconds less, and the standing quarter-mile over one second less than with the Victor tested in 1957. Maximum speed, too, is higher by some 1½ m.p.h. There has been a small increase in power output—54.8 b.h.p. gross at 4,200 r.p.m., compared with 52 b.h.p. at the same speed, but the weight of the De Luxe test car was about 1 cwt greater. Gear ratios and tyre sizes remain the same.

Left: Switches for ignition, starter, wipers (and screen wash), side and head lights, interior and facia lights are combined, in three controls on the right of the driver. Right: Separate front seats, leather trimmed over latex foam with a helical spring base are comfortable and give good support

The 1,507 c.c., four-cylinder engine is a smooth unit which remains quiet throughout the speed range. It becomes noticeable to the passengers because of some body resonance at between 46 and 60 m.p.h. in top, and when accelerating hard in the indirect gears. Although the car is generally very tractable, there is some roughness when pulling below 28 m.p.h. in top so that, although it is possible to accelerate from as low as 12 m.p.h. in this gear, the feeling is much happier if a down change to second is made when speed is checked in a built-up area. Second is a very useful gear for overtaking, maximum torque corresponding to about 30 m.p.h. in this ratio, and 40 to 45 m.p.h. can be used regularly as a maximum. For continuous cruising, 65 m.p.h. (speedometer 69) is a comfortable speed which avoids the slight resonance and does not seem to be overstressing the engine.

The ride is quieter than in earlier Victors. In all probability a carpeted floor has helped in this respect. At low speeds, however, the suspension feels harsh, particularly when lightly laden, with some noise also coming through from the suspension. At higher speeds, this tends to become smoothed out, and a stable, pitch-free ride is enjoyed.

Fully laden, the ride is much improved. Body drum is not pronounced over cobbles, but there are body tremors and high-frequency reaction through the steering. These remarks apply also to poorer road surfaces other than cobbles. Against this, the Victor has a pleasant, solid feeling on the road, and considerable sensitiveness in its controls. Although it rolls to some extent on corners, the quickly responsive steering enables the car to be placed accurately and held on its line. Steering characteristics are almost neutral—with a slight bias towards understeer—which is cancelled out when fully laden. A little more rear wheel adhesion would be welcomed when cornering fast on wet roads. Tyre squeal is almost entirely absent.

Steering is light in normal driving with no lost motion, and there is plenty of feel in the steering which gives an indication of the state of the road surface. There is strong self-centring action; low speed manoeuvring is easy, helped by the small turning circle.

The brakes are first-class on the Victor. They are light to operate, sensitive and progressive in action, and there is no roughness when applied hard from high speeds. They had ample power for an emergency stop, pulled the car up squarely and did not cause the rear wheels to lock first when in the laden test condition. During normal fast driving, they showed no fade.

Wind noise is low, and the narrow pivoting ventilators in the front door windows can be opened to a position in which whistle is avoided, yet air is extracted without draughts. These vents, which have a thief-proof catch, were prevented from opening easily by the rubber sealing at their edges. All windows winders work with a light yet rapid action, and the windows can be lowered completely into the doors. The doors are well sealed against draughts, and do not require heavy slamming to close them. Internal handles have to be lifted to release the catches as a safeguard against unintentional opening. Burst catches, consisting of interlocking channels on door edge and pillar, minimise the risk of doors being forced open in an accident.

A powerful heater (an optional extra) was fitted on the test car. Although temperatures were low at times during the test, it was never found necessary to bring the booster fan into operation. When required, this fan can be run at one of two speeds by moving a three-position switch beneath the centre of the facia. Controls for heat and air consist of a pair of small levers placed beside the central ashtray. A flap on the body of the heater unit can be opened by the driver to admit extra cold air in hot weather. With this flap open, and the fresh air intake closed, recirculatory heating can be obtained. There is no separate control over demisting, a proportion of air leaving the heater being ducted to the screen.

Instruments are in a cowled panel ahead of the driver, which prevents reflections in the screen at night. The scale of the rather vague and optimistic speedometer fills this panel, with the remaining instruments, consisting of a water thermometer and fuel gauge, inset in the face. A total mileage recorder is at the centre, magnified by a lens. Warning lights for ignition, oil pressure, flashing indicators and head lamp main beam are also in this panel. A powerful horn with a good quality note is operated by a half horn ring. Head lights have an adequate reach and good spread, and are controlled by a pull-out switch on the right of the facia. This switch also operates the roof light, and a panel light

Amber turn indicators are mounted high up and clear of the tail and stop lamps and reflectors to avoid confusion of signals. Bright parts above the waist are polished stainless steel

rheostat when rotated. The roof light is also switched on when the front doors are opened. A manually-tuned radio was installed—an optional extra; it gave moderately good reception and was reasonably selective. The tuning panel lighting was too bright at night. A clock with concealed lighting, also controlled by the rheostat, was mounted above the screen between the sun vizors.

For all ordinary purposes the Series 2 Victor is a 30 m.p.g. car and therefore a safe range of over 200 miles is given by the 8-gallon fuel tank. Although the filler behind the hinged panel in the left rear wing has been re-positioned at a better angle for filling, it is easy to catch a thumb between the eared cap and the edge of the opening. With ignition set as on the test car, there is slight pinking when pulling hard on premium fuel, and running is not very satisfactory on a premium/standard grade mixture.

The counterbalanced bonnet lid has been modified to open to a higher position, making it easier to work beneath the down-turned front edge. It is released by a catch in front of the grille, and has no primary control within the car. Of exceptional depth for a car of this size, the boot also has a counterbalanced lid and carries the spare wheel vertically in a well to the right of the floor. In this position, it can be removed quickly without disturbing luggage. There is no means of opening the boot without using the ignition key, and this proved to be rather tiresome when frequent access to the boot was required. The interior is partially illuminated at night by the number plate lamp on the rear bumper.

This test confirms that much development work and attention to detail have gone into the Victor since its introduction. Refinement, both in mechanical behaviour and body finish, are much improved, and performance is enhanced. Separate front seats and the superior comfort and appointments of the De Luxe car are certainly worth the extra money, which amounts to £35 (£52 10s including P.T.), compared with the Victor Super. It is a compact but roomy four-seater, with very large luggage locker; it is quite lively and economical, and easy to drive. Handling qualities are above average in its class, and it has good brakes. This Victor is a very satisfactory choice for family motoring, and it has behind it the world-wide General Motors servicing organization.

VAUXHALL VICTOR DE LUXE SERIES 2

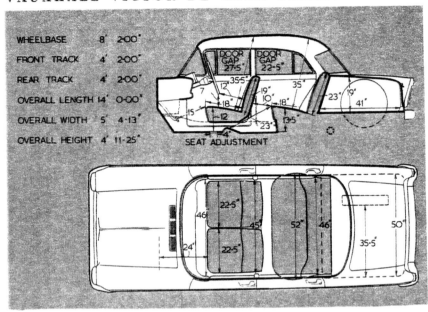

Scale ⅛in to 1ft. Driving seat in central position. Cushions uncompressed.

PERFORMANCE

ACCELERATION:
Speed Range, Gear Ratios and Time in sec.

M.P.H.	4.12 to 1	6.74 to 1	13.14 to 1
10—30	11.9	6.7	—
20—40	11.7	7.3	—
30—50	14.3	9.7	—
40—60	18.6	—	—

From rest through gears to:

M.P.H.	sec.
30	6.4
40	10.3
50	15.5
60	28.1

Standing quarter mile 22.8 sec.

MAXIMUM SPEEDS ON GEARS:

Gear	M.P.H.	K.P.H.
Top (mean)	76.4	122.9
(best)	80.0	128.7
2nd	55	88.5
1st	28	45.0

TRACTIVE EFFORT:

	Pull (lb per ton)	Equivalent Gradient
Top	218	1 in 10.2
Second	362	1 in 6.1

BRAKES (at 30 m.p.h. in neutral):

Pedal load in lb	Retardation	Equivalent stopping distance in ft
25	0.17g	178
50	0.42g	72
75	0.60g	50
100	0.88g	34.3

FUEL CONSUMPTION:
M.P.G. at steady speeds

M.P.H.	Direct Top
30	44.0
40	38.5
50	33.9
60	30.3
70	25.6

Overall fuel consumption for 1,046 miles, 28.1 m.p.g. (10.1 litres per 100 km).
Approximate normal range 27-37 m.p.g. (10.5-7.6 litres per 100 km).
Fuel: Premium grade.

TEST CONDITIONS: Weather: dry, overcast. Tarmacadam surface. 6-8 m.p.h. wind. Air temperature 37 deg. F.
Acceleration figures are the mean of several runs in opposite directions.
Tractive effort obtained by Tapley meter.

SPEEDOMETER CORRECTION: M.P.H.

Car speedometer:	10	20	30	40	50	60	70	80
True speed:	10	19	28	37	46.5	56	66	75

DATA

PRICE (basic), with saloon body, £565.
British purchase tax, £283 17s.
Total (in Great Britain), £848 17s.
Extras: Radio £15 12s 6d plus £5 13s purchase tax.
Heater £14 15s including purchase tax.

ENGINE: Capacity: 1,507 c.c. (92 cu in).
Number of cylinders: 4.
Bore and stroke: 79.4 × 76.2 mm (3.125 × 3in).
Valve gear: o.h.v. pushrods.
Compression ratio: 7.8 to 1.
B.H.P.: 54.8 (gross) at 4,200 r.p.m. (B.H.P. per ton laden 46.6).
Torque: 84.5lb ft at 2,400 r.p.m.
M.P.H. per 1,000 r.p.m. in top gear: 16.5.

WEIGHT (with 5 gal fuel): 20.6 cwt (2,303lb).
Weight distribution (per cent): F, 55.6; R, 44.4.
Laden as tested: 23.6 cwt (2,639 lb).
Lb per c.c. (laden): 1.75.

BRAKES: Type: Lockheed.
Method of operation: Hydraulic.
Drum dimensions: Front and rear, 8in diameter; 1.5in wide.
Lining area: F, 46 sq in; R, 46 sq in (78.2 sq in per ton laden).

TYRES: 5.60—13in Firestone de luxe tubeless.
Pressures (lb sq in): F, 24; R, 24 (normal).

TANK CAPACITY: 8 Imperial gallons.
Oil sump: 7.5 pints.
Cooling system: 10.5 pints (plus 1.5 pints if heater fitted).

STEERING: Turning circle:
Between kerbs, 33ft 4in L; 33ft R.
Between walls, 35ft 6in L; 35ft R.
Turns of steering wheel from lock to lock: 3.75.

DIMENSIONS: Wheelbase: 8ft 2in.
Track: F, 4ft 2in; R, 4ft 2in.
Length (overall): 14ft.
Width: 5ft 4.13in.
Height: 4ft 11.25in.
Ground clearance: 6.35in.
Frontal area: 19.5 sq ft (approximately).

ELECTRICAL SYSTEM: 12-volt; 43 ampere-hour battery.
Head lights: Double dip; 40-50 watt bulbs.

SUSPENSION: Front, independent, coil springs and wishbones, anti-roll bar. Rear, live axle and semi-elliptic springs.

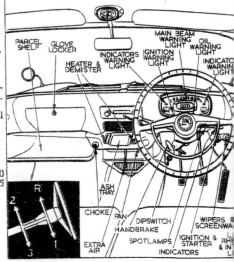

The Motor ROAD TESTS

The Vauxhall Victor Estate Car

SMART and practical, the Victor Estate Car retains the very good handling and roadholding qualities of the saloon version. Among the optional extras fitted to the test car were twin auxiliary lamps, heater, radio, screen-washers and two-pedal control.

A 1½-litre Car with Great Carrying Power, Tested with Two-pedal Control

IT is common for estate car, or utility, versions of popular saloon models to offer increased carrying power at the cost of greater size and higher weight, with which are coupled lower maximum speed, reduced acceleration and hill climbing power, and poorer fuel consumption. It is also not unusual that the harder suspension required to cope with the additional load results in a noticeably harsher ride over rough surfaces.

Extended tests with the Vauxhall Victor Estate Car show that few of these penalties are exacted in return for a 50% increase in baggage-carrying power when the car is normally used as a four- or five-seater, and double the normal luggage-carrying capacity when the rear seat and squab are folded forward to give a maximum permissible load of 850 lb. disposed in 45 cu. ft.

As compared with the standard saloon these changes are made within an unchanged framework of space and at a cost of only 55 lb. (or 2%) in weight. In order however to cope with a considerably higher potential all-up weight, the section of the tyres is increased and the gear ratio altered so that the car moves at 14.7 m.p.h. at 1,000 r.p.m. whereas the standard saloon model does 16.5 m.p.h. at the same engine speed. As one might expect, when driven in normal trim with only two up this lower top gear ratio, in conjunction with almost unchanged all-up weight, results in improved acceleration, the elapsed time between 20 and 40 m.p.h. being brought down from 12.5 to 10.7 seconds and the stiffest gradient climbable in top gear improving from 1 in 13.5 to 1 in 10.7.

What is somewhat surprising is that neither this lower top gear, nor the sloping but flat tail which ends the rectangular shape of the body sides and roof, has impaired performance at the upper end of the speed range; on the contrary, the acceleration time between 40 and 60 m.p.h. comes down from 19 seconds to 18.6 seconds and the maximum speed goes up from 74.4 to 76.8 m.p.h. In only one basic, and another ancillary, aspect does the Estate Car show to disadvantage (apart from the not unimportant extra £100 in ex-works price) which is in respect of fuel consumption which falls off from 30.6 to 25.8 m.p.g. presumably as a consequence of continuously higher engine speed. Acceleration through the gears is slightly impaired following the use on the car tested of a clutchless gear change which slows down the shifting process.

As is now commonly known, on the Newton two-pedal control a touch on the gear lever excites an electric circuit which opens valves exposing a servo piston to vacuum induced in the engine manifold. By this means the clutch is withdrawn during the gear-change period, the throttle being simultaneously slightly opened so as to diminish the load on the synchronizing cones which are fitted between all three ratios on the Vauxhall gearbox. This throttle bias also ensures that when the driver removes pressure from the gear lever, and thus releases the vacuum withdrawal mechanism, the clutch will positively return into action under the guidance of the centrifugal weights which bring it into engagement at over 800 r.p.m.

When the engine is idling, return springs release the friction surfaces so that when a gear is engaged the car does not move forward. The arrangement gives complete two-pedal control with genuine simplicity and a number of safeguards against failure which include a method of locking the clutch so that the engine is effective as a brake when a gear is engaged with the car stationary, a legal requirement in some countries. The price is very moderate for what many drivers will consider a real convenience, but it must be admitted that on the car tested the operation in some respects left something to be desired. Smooth take-ups from rest on the level required careful work on the accelerator and unless the handbrake was used as a damper, surge-free forward and backward movements such as are necessary with close parking were impossible to achieve.

In Brief
Price (including two-pedal control as tested) £637 plus purchase tax £319 17s. equals £956 17s.
Price with normal clutch (including purchase tax) £931 7s.
Capacity ... ... 1,507 c.c.
Unladen kerb weight ... 21 cwt.
Acceleration:
  20-40 m.p.h. in top gear ... 10.7 sec.
  0-50 m.p.h. through gears 21.4 sec.
Maximum direct top-gear gradient ... ... 1 in 10.7
Maximum speed ... 76.8 m.p.h.
"Maximile" speed ... 75.6 m.p.h.
Touring fuel consumption ... 32 m.p.g.
Gearing: 14.7 m.p.h. in top gear at 1,000 r.p.m.; 29.4 m.p.h. at 1,000 ft./min. piston speed.

The Motor ROAD TESTS
The Motor Road Test No. 25/58

Make: Vauxhall
Type: Victor Estate Car (with 2-pedal control)
Makers: Vauxhall Motors, Ltd., Luton, Beds.

Test Data

World copyright reserved; no unauthorized reproduction in whole or in part

CONDITIONS: Weather: Dry, wind speed 3-7 m.p.h. (Temperature 69°-76°F., Barometer 29.84 to 29.93 in. Hg.). Surface: Dry tarmacadam. Fuel: Premium grade pump petrol (approx. 95 Research Method Octane Rating).

INSTRUMENTS
Speedometer at 30 m.p.h. .. .. 8% fast
Speedometer at 60 m.p.h. .. .. 6% fast
Distance recorder .. .. 4% fast

WEIGHT
Kerb weight (unladen, but with oil, coolant and fuel for approx. 50 miles) .. 21 cwt.
Front/rear distribution of kerb weight 56/44
Weight laden as tested .. .. 24.5 cwt.

MAXIMUM SPEEDS
Flying Quarter Mile
Mean of four opposite runs.. .. 76.8 m.p.h.
Best one-way time equals .. 78.8 m.p.h.

"Maximile" Speed. (Timed quarter mile after one mile accelerating from rest.)
Mean of four opposite runs .. 75.6 m.p.h.
Best one-way time equals .. 76.4 m.p.h.

Speed in gears
Max. speed in 2nd gear .. .. 50 m.p.h.
Max. speed in 1st gear .. .. 26 m.p.h.

FUEL CONSUMPTION
(Direct top gear)
43.5 m.p.g. at constant 30 m.p.h. on level.
40.0 m.p.g. at constant 40 m.p.h. on level.
36.0 m.p.g. at constant 50 m.p.h. on level.
31.0 m.p.g. at constant 60 m.p.h. on level.
23.0 m.p.g. at constant 70 m.p.h. on level.

Overall Fuel Consumption for 664 miles, 25¾ gallons, equals 25.8 m.p.g. (10.8 litres/100 km.)
Touring Fuel Consumption (m.p.g. at steady speed midway between 30 m.p.h. and maximum, less 5% allowance for acceleration) 32.0 m.p.g.
Fuel tank capacity (maker's figure) .. 8 gallons

STEERING
Turning circle between kerbs:
Left .. .. 31¼ feet
Right .. .. 31¼ feet
Turns of steering wheel from lock to lock 3¾

BRAKES from 30 m.p.h.
0.95g retardation (equivalent to 31¼ ft. stopping distance) with 90 lb. pedal pressure
0.85g retardation (equivalent to 35½ ft. stopping distance) with 75 lb. pedal pressure
0.55g retardation (equivalent to 54½ ft. stopping distance) with 50 lb. pedal pressure
0.34g retardation (equivalent to 88 ft. stopping distance) with 25 lb. pedal pressure

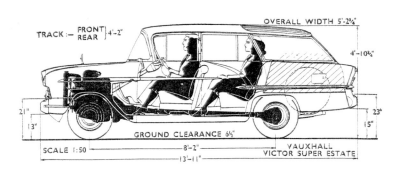

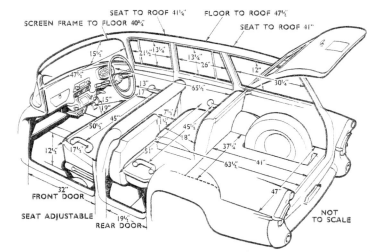

ACCELERATION TIMES from standstill
0-30 m.p.h. .. .. 9.0 sec.
0-40 m.p.h. .. .. 12.1 sec.
0-50 m.p.h. .. .. 21.4 sec.
0-60 m.p.h. .. .. 30.3 sec.
0-70 m.p.h. .. .. 52.6 sec.
Standing quarter mile .. 25.4 sec.

ACCELERATION TIMES on Upper Ratios
	Top gear	2nd gear
10-30 m.p.h.	11.6 sec.	7.2 sec.
20-40 m.p.h.	10.7 sec.	8.4 sec.
30-50 m.p.h.	14.7 sec.	11.4 sec.
40-60 m.p.h.	18.5 sec.	—
50-70 m.p.h.	30.5 sec.	—

HILL CLIMBING at sustained steady speeds
Max. gradient on top gear .. 1 in 10.7 (Tapley 210 lb./ton)
Max. gradient on 2nd gear .. 1 in 6.7 (Tapley 330 lb./ton)

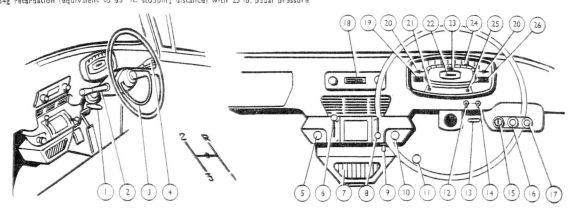

1, Handbrake. 2, Gear lever. 3, Horn ring. 4, Direction indicator switch. 5, Choke control. 6, Ventilator control. 7, Heater. 8, Heater control. 9, Heater fan switch. 10, Blank (optional cigar lighter). 11, Headlamp dip switch. 12, 14, Fog lamp switches. 13, Clutch lock (tow-start). 15, Ignition and starter switch. 16, Windscreen wiper control. 17, Lights switch (inst. panel and interior lights). 18, Radio. 19, Water thermometer. 20, Direction indicator warning light. 21, Dynamo charge warning light. 22, Distance recorder. 23, Headlamp high-beam indicator lamp. 24, Speedometer. 25, Oil pressure warning light. 26, Fuel contents gauge.

The Vauxhall Victor Estate Ca

MOST modern dual-purpose cars retain the normal four-door saloon amenities in their estate-car form, and the Victor is no exception, as is evident on the left. Occupants have extremely good all-round visibility, but the projecting base of the wrapround windscreen can bruise the knees of those entering the front compartment. As can be seen on the right, even with all seats ready for use there remains a sizeable luggage platform, at a sensible level for loading and reached through a large, counter-balanced door.

Generally speaking the gear changes themselves were smoothly effected but on downward changes the driver could make a useful contribution by opening the throttle and when changing up it was desirable to take one's foot off the accelerator. It is for this specific reason that the standing start through-the-gears acceleration figures compare unfavourably with the standard model, but the loss in performance is not of a kind which would be noticed in normal motoring, and although the system is far from foolproof it gives satisfactory results with normal intelligence and co-operation and makes driving easier, particularly in traffic as a consequence of reduced physical effort.

The driver is ill advised to take advantage of the fact that the car can be started on the level in top gear, for this procedure will almost certainly reduce the life of the clutch plate; smoother starts can be made in second gear than in bottom, but for clutch longevity this practice is not advised. With excellent torque in the lower speed ranges, and a genuinely smooth engine, the car operates effectively without gear changing from 20 m.p.h. upwards; although 50 m.p.h. can be reached in second gear if necessary, 40 m.p.h. on this ratio would not normally be exceeded.

Turning now to those qualities which will be found in the car, irrespective of which transmission system the owner chooses, a 25% increase in the stiffness of the rear springs seems to have enhanced the cornering powers which were an outstandingly good feature of the saloon. Roll when cornering is reduced but slight under-steer remains, so that the car can be driven through corners in a stable condition, which is acceptable to passengers at a speed perhaps 10 m.p.h. higher than is normal for this class of car. There is some deterioration in passenger comfort over really rough roads as a consequence of this stiffer springing and some shake can be noticed in the hull structure if in these conditions one forces the car along at between, say, 45 and 60 m.p.h. On the other hand the car rides well over rough tracks at moderate speeds and is therefore quite suitable for use over typical farm roads, or even open country.

The rear seat easily swings over, exposing the tool kit beneath it, and a simple latch then permits the squab to be moved through rather more than 90° to give a flat solid floor at the base of the vehicle to which access is easily made through the tail gate which swings up on spring counter-balances after the lock has been released. Objects slightly longer than 5 feet and up to 3 feet wide can be accom-

STRONGLY counterbalanced, the bonnet of the Victor can be lifted with little effort but could well open wider for easy access. Accessibility of battery, distributor, carburetter, plugs, dynamo and valvegear is good, but the coil and fuel pump are not easily reached.

modated on this floor and loading is eased by the fact that it is only 2 feet from the ground.

Rear seat passengers also may enter or leave with ease but those in front may be obstructed by the cranked-back pillar for the panoramic windscreen There seems little, if any, gain in visibility through this form of screen, although both driver and passenger do enjoy an excellent view marred only by the inability of the two "clap hands" wiper blades to clear the width of the glass effectively from rain and mud.

The arcuate speedometer dial is easy to read, and the switch gear is well styled, although it is too much perhaps to ask one switch effectively to control the side, head, interior lights, and instrument lighting.

Forward of the screen the bonnet opens through a pitifully inadequate angle, making access to anything beneath it an awkward physical feat. That the makers have a somewhat contemptuous attitude to owner-driver maintenance is shown by the way in which both the coil and the fuel pump are hidden beneath the steering box on right-hand-drive cars, and as it is recommended that the pump be dismantled every 5,000 miles this is not a point that can readily be overlooked. Nor indeed can the rear axle noise which was prominent at high speeds, partly one supposes due to the absence of the usual sealed-off luggage compartment.

The high noise level in the heating and de-misting system which has a two-speed fan, can be excused in the light of the immense air blast, which might prove invaluable in extreme conditions, and similarly the poor quality of the noise coming from the radio set can be forgiven because of the very low price of the set offered by the car manufacturers.

Attention must be drawn to the very wide range of other optional extras which are set out in our list, there being much in favour of this policy of cataloguing a car with a somewhat austere interior and leaving it to the owner to choose what items he most desires to embellish it.

The Victor however certainly contains all the elements that are needed for satisfactory motoring, from the distinctive exterior to the well-planned interior which includes comfortable rear seats. Although the knee room is little over 7 inches when the front seat is fully back, the passengers' feet may easily be placed beneath it.

The front seat itself would be improved by a higher squab to give better support to the shoulders, and the front armrests are not ideally positioned. On the other hand the convenience of the front passenger is well looked after by a deep glove locker on the left hand side of the scuttle which may at option be fitted with both a lock and an interior light, and supplemented by an optional parcel shelf immediately below it.

The Estate Car is built to the "Super" specification which includes a chromium-plated horn ring on the two-spoke steering wheel; armrests on all the side doors; an ashtray for the rear seat passengers; twin sun vizors and stainless steel surrounds for the windscreen, side windows and the rear window. A further item of Super specification is the projection of the exhaust pipe through the right-hand side of the rear bumper, but judging by the corrosion caused by the products of combustion it may be doubted whether this last feature is an advantage.

With the exception of some items of maintenance, all the practical features required in the motorcar in general, and the estate type in particular, are very well taken care of in this latest contribution of the British industry. When to this one adds maximum speed well above 75 m.p.h., exceptional handling qualities which make driving a real pleasure, reasonable fuel consumption, and a basic price which leaves some substantial change out of £1,000 (even when purchase tax has been paid) one has a most attractive proposition for anyone who must combine business with pleasure, or whose pleasure is coupled with the carriage of loads considerably beyond the capacity of the normal four-door saloon.

Specification

Engine
- Cylinders ... 4
- Bore ... 79.37 mm.
- Stroke ... 76.2 mm.
- Cubic capacity ... 1,507 c.c.
- Piston area ... 30.7 sq. in.
- Valves ... Overhead, pushrod
- Compression ratio ... 7.8/1
- Carburetter ... Zenith 34VN
- Fuel pump ... AC mechanical
- Ignition timing control and vacuum ... Centrifugal
- Oil filter ... AC by-pass
- Max. power (gross/net) ... 54.8/48.5 b.h.p.
- at ... 4,200 r.p.m.
- Piston speed at max. b.h.p. 2,100 ft./min.

Transmission
- Clutch ... Borg and Beck
- Top gear (s/m) ... 4.625
- 2nd gear (s/m) ... 7.562
- 1st gear (s/m) ... 14.735
- Reverse ... 14.106
- Propeller shaft ... Hardy Spicer open
- Final drive ... Hypoid bevel
- Top gear m.p.h. at 1,000 r.p.m. 14.7
- Top gear m.p.h. at 1,000 ft./min. piston speed ... 29.4

Chassis
- Brakes ... Vauxhall-Lockheed hydraulic
- Brake drum internal diameter ... 8 in.
- Friction lining area ... 92 sq. in.
- Suspension:
  - Front ... Coil and wishbone
  - Rear ... Semi-elliptic
- Shock absorbers:
  - Front ... Telescopic
  - Rear ... Telescopic
- Steering gear ... Burman re-circulating ball
- Tyres ... 5.90—13

Coachwork and Equipment

- Starting handle ... None
- Battery mounting ... Beneath bonnet
- Jack ... Scissor type
- Jacking points ... 2 in front of rear wheels, 2 behind front wheels
- Standard tool kit: Jack, wheelnut spanner, 1 spanner ¼-7/16 s.a.e., 1 spanner ⅜-7/16 s.a.e., sparking plug spanner, brake adjustment spanner, screwdriver, 7 in. adjustable spanner.
- Exterior lights: 2 head, 2 side, 2 tail, 2 brake, 1 number plate light.
- Number of electrical fuses ... 2 line fuses, 2 thermal interrupters
- Direction indicators ... Flashing type
- Windscreen wipers ... Dual two-speed electric self cancelling
- Windscreen washers ... Optional
- Sun vizors ... Two
- Instruments: Speedometer with decimal trip, fuel gauge, water temperature gauge.
- Warning lights: Oil pressure, dynamo charge and main beam

- Locks:
  - With ignition key ... Front doors and boot
  - With other keys ... None
- Glove lockers ... 1 in facia
- Map pockets ... None
- Parcel shelves ... Optional
- Ashtrays ... 1 in facia, 1 behind front seat
- Cigar lighters ... None
- Interior lights ... 1
- Interior heater ... Optional
- Car radio ... Optional
- Extras available: Radio, heater, parcel shelf, bonnet emblem, spare wheel cover, towing attachment, floor mats, reversing light, sun vizor, screen washer, seat covers, rear compartment mat, and other fitments set out in maker's approved accessory list.
- Upholstery material ... Elastofab
- Floor covering ... Rubber mats
- Exterior colours standardized .. 5 single, 4 dual
- Alternative body styles ... 4-door saloon

Maintenance

- Sump ... 7½ pints, S.A.E. 20
- Gearbox ... 2 pints, S.A.E. 90
- Rear axle ... 2½ pints, S.A.E. 90
- Steering gear lubricant ... 90 S.A.E.
- Cooling system capacity ... 10½ pints (2 drain taps)
- Chassis lubrication ... By oil gun every 1,000 miles to 17 points
- Ignition timing ... 9° b.t.d.c.
- Contact-breaker gap ... 0.019/0.021
- Sparking plug type ... AC 45/5V
- Sparking plug gap ... 0.028
- Valve timing: Inlet opens 19.6° b.t.d.c., inlet closes 60.6° a.b.d.c., exhaust opens 51.6° b.b.d.c., exhaust closes 38.6° a.t.d.c.
- Tappet clearances (hot):
  - Inlet ... 0.013 in.
  - Exhaust ... 0.013 in.
- Front wheel toe-in ... 0.125
- Camber angle ... 0° 38'
- Castor angle ... 1° 30'
- Steering swivel pin inclination ... 4°
- Tyre pressures:
  - Front ... 24 lb.
  - Rear ... 24 lb. (30 lb. fully laden)
- Brake fluid ... Lockheed No. 33
- Battery type and capacity ... Exide 12 v. 43 amp.hr.

The Motor ROAD TESTS
The Vauxhall Victor Series 2 De Luxe

Simplified Styling Matched by Much Improved Quality and Performance

Clean-lined and less adorned, the Victor retains all its useful dimensions. The luggage shown (right) left plenty of space in the boot; only a matter of an inch or so prevented another of the large cases being installed.

COMMENTS on styling are ordinarily out of place in a road test report, in which fact must take precedence over opinion. In the case of the Series 2 Vauxhall Victor some reference to styling is inevitable, for there can be little doubt that the Victor as it was first revealed two years ago was so controversial in appearance that many people never even attempted to try its good qualities. By comparison the latest model looks more "ordinary"; a change which should have the beneficial result of introducing to a wider public a car that has been improved at the same time in a large number of minor ways with a major overall result.

The de luxe model which is the subject of this report is an addition to the Victor range. Costing £90 more than the cheapest of the three variants, including British purchase tax, it offers a dual colour scheme, refinements of trim and the more significant luxury of well-shaped individual front seats. The sound sense of this last item—the Victor being in all respects a four-seater without compromise—underlines a thoughtful approach which may come as a surprise to those who imagine designers and stylists unable to work in harmony. First impressions of the new Victor suggest a sensible, lightly-handling family saloon. Further acquaintance not only reinforces these impressions but reveals many of the practical details which spring from hard thinking and hard development work.

Cars from the Luton factory have been described, sometimes a little unkindly, as the nearest thing to "painless" motoring. The latest example can claim with justification to have eliminated the pain without removing the pleasure, re-establishing a Vauxhall standard of silence and easy performance in a 1½-litre saloon which is at the same time unusually responsive to the demands of a keen driver. To consider the comfortable aspect first, it should go on record that the Victor was one of the most untiring of orthodox cars to drive on a long journey which has come the way of The Motor for some time. How much of the credit for this should go to the suspension and how much to the seats is not easy to decide. Conventional on paper, the suspension with its very long, asymmetric leaf rear springs is better at absorbing really bad bumps of the semi-colonial road type than it is at concealing altogether the small imperfections of an English main road. The damping is excellent in avoiding the floating ride characteristic of some softly sprung cars, while quite pronounced cornering roll which is exaggerated by a high driving position and a high bonnet is made less troublesome by seats providing good lateral support. On the other hand even a sponge rubber overlay on the upholstery does not prevent lightweight passengers from being bounced up and down if the car is hustled over minor roads.

Dimensions tell some of the story but not all. Without being exceptionally large in any direction internally, the Victor uses the space to the best advantage of its allotted four occupants. Six-foot drivers will appreciate a seat which can be slid

In Brief
Price £565 plus purchase tax £283 17s. equals £848 17s.	
Capacity	1,507 c.c.
Unladen kerb weight	20¼ cwt.
Acceleration:	
20-40 m.p.h. in top gear	10.1 sec.
0-50 m.p.h. through gears	16.0 sec.
Maximum direct top gear gradient	1 in 10.6
Maximum speed	75.3 m.p.h.
"Maximile" speed	74.4 m.p.h.
Touring fuel consumption	29.1 m.p.g.
Gearing: 16.3 m.p.h. in top gear at 1,000 r.p.m.; 32.6 m.p.h. at 1,000 ft./min. piston speed.	

11

The Motor Road Test No. 7/59

Make: Vauxhall **Type:** Victor Series 2 De Luxe
Makers: Vauxhall Motors, Ltd., Luton, Beds.

Test Data

World copyright reserved; no unauthorized reproduction in whole or in part.

CONDITIONS: Weather: Dry, little wind. (Temperature 38°, 46° F., Barometer 30.1 in. Hg.). Surface: Dry tarmac. Fuel: British premium grade pump petrol (approx. 95 Research Method Octane Rating).

INSTRUMENTS
Speedometer at 30 m.p.h. .. .. 9% fast
Speedometer at 60 m.p.h. .. .. 4% fast
Distance recorder .. .. 2½% fast

WEIGHT
Kerb weight (unladen, but with oil, coolant and fuel for approx. 50 miles) .. 20 cwt.
Front/rear distribution of kerb weight 56/44
Weight laden as tested .. 23¾ cwt.

MAXIMUM SPEEDS
Flying Quarter Mile
Mean of four opposite runs .. .. 75.3 m.p.h.
Best one-way time equals .. .. 78.2 m.p.h.

"Maximile" Speed. (Timed quarter mile after one mile accelerating from rest.)
Mean of four opposite runs .. .. 74.4 m.p.h.
Best one-way time equals .. .. 76.3 m.p.h.

Speed in gears
Max. speed in 2nd gear .. .. 52 m.p.h.
Max. speed in 1st gear .. .. 28 m.p.h.

FUEL CONSUMPTION
41¼ m.p.g. at constant 30 m.p.h. on level.
36¼ m.p.g. at constant 40 m.p.h. on level.
31¼ m.p.g. at constant 50 m.p.h. on level.
28 m.p.g. at constant 60 m.p.h. on level.
23 m.p.g. at constant 70 m.p.h. on level.

Overall Fuel Consumption for 1,306 miles, 49.6 gallons, equals 26.3 m.p.g. (10.75 litres/100 km.)

Touring Fuel Consumption (m.p.g. at steady speed midway between 30 m.p.h. and maximum, less 5% allowance for acceleration) 29.1 m.p.g.

Fuel Tank Capacity (maker's figure) 8 gallons.

STEERING
Turning circle between kerbs:
Left .. .. 31¼ feet
Right .. .. 31 feet
Turns of steering wheel from lock to lock 3¾

BRAKES from 30 m.p.h.
0.90 g retardation (equivalent to 33½ ft. stopping distance) with 85 lb. pedal pressure.
0.87 g retardation (equivalent to 34½ ft. stopping distance) with 75 lb. pedal pressure.
0.62 g retardation (equivalent to 48½ ft. stopping distance) with 50 lb. pedal pressure.
0.28 g retardation (equivalent to 107½ ft. stopping distance) with 25 lb. pedal pressure.

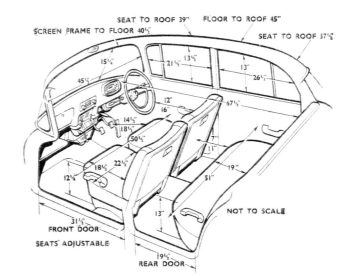

ACCELERATION TIMES from standstill
0-30 m.p.h. .. .. 5.9 sec.
0-40 m.p.h. .. .. 9.4 sec.
0-50 m.p.h. .. .. 16.0 sec.
0-60 m.p.h. .. .. 24.8 sec.
0-70 m.p.h. .. .. 40.6 sec.
Standing quarter mile .. 22.7 sec.

ACCELERATION TIMES on upper ratios
	Top gear	2nd gear
10-30 m.p.h.	10.3 sec.	5.7 sec.
20-40 m.p.h.	10.1 sec.	6.6 sec.
30-50 m.p.h.	12.6 sec.	8.9 sec.
40-60 m.p.h.	16.3 sec.	—
50-70 m.p.h.	22.9 sec.	—

HILL CLIMBING at sustained steady speeds
Max. gradient on top gear .. 1 in 10.6 (Tapley 190 lb./ton)
Max. gradient on 2nd gear .. 1 in 6.3 (Tapley 350 lb./ton)

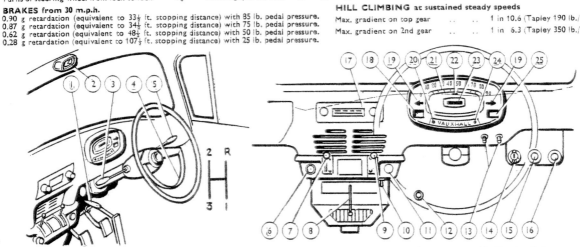

1, Handbrake. 2, Clock. 3, Gear lever. 4, Horn ring. 5, Direction indicator switch. 6, Choke control. 7, Heater and ventilator air intake control. 8, Cold air intake control. 9, Heater temperature control. 10, Heater fan switch. 11, Cigar lighter (optional extra). 12, Headlamp dip switch. 13, Switches for auxiliary lamps (when fitted). 14, Ignition, starter and auxiliary circuit switch. 15, Windscreen wipers and washers switch. 16, Lights, facia rheostat and interior light switch. 17, Radio controls. 18, Water thermometer. 19, Direction indicator warning light. 20, Dynamo charge warning light. 21, Speedometer. 22, Main beam indicator light. 23, Distance recorder. 24, Oil pressure warning light. 25, Fuel contents gauge.

The Vauxhall Victor Series 2 De Luxe

The de luxe model is distinguished by leather upholstery, special trim and two very comfortable separate front seats. The heater, radio and parcel shelf shown in this picture are optional extras.

back to an almost straight-legged position and provision for altering both height and angle by means of pads. There is an elbow-rest for everybody, including the driver who can make use of it when he wants to without being obstructed at critical moments.

Equally important for long-distance comfort is a rare combination of silence and ventilation which makes it possible, at 65 m.p.h., to listen without straining to a radio of only middling quality, yet stay warm and well provided with fresh air. Heaters are so much a *sine qua non* of today's motoring that no excuse is offered for mentioning an optional accessory; controlled by two sliding knobs and a two-speed fan switch, it allows instant mixing of hot and cold fresh air in any proportion (but without differentiating between the demisting and heater outlets), or can be used with a very noisy booster fan to recirculate air when the atmosphere outside contains fumes or dust. Presumably through maladjustment, the unit on the test car would not produce completely cold air. Hinged flaps in the front windows ventilate without draught once force or ingenuity has been applied to open them, and in the half-open position create very little wind noise. Great pains have obviously been taken to ensure silence, the engine being exceptionally quiet for a car of this class, while drumming in the body is not apparent until just above the 65 m.p.h. cruising speed quoted previously.

Visibility is an awkward quantity to measure. The full wrap-around windscreen is a design which is apt to arouse prejudice, but it is probably fair to say that for most people the forward view from the driving seat of most objects which affect safety—that is anything from the level of the driver's eyes downwards—is better than normal. Conversely, an overhanging roof causes such things as treetops and close-up traffic lights to disappear from sight earlier, while the best compromise achieved by two windscreen wiper blades swinging in opposition leaves blind triangles at both ends and in the middle of the screen. A three-bladed wiper might offer the solution—its use is not unknown. Sideways and to the rear the visibility is good, including a view of all four wings for parking.

Some of *The Motor's* staff struck the corner of the windscreen pillar with their knee occasionally when getting in, some did it always and some never. Once installed, the driver is well set up to take advantage of the Victor's dual personality, driving lazily with infrequent changes of gear or using positive controls and good road-holding to enjoy himself. Modest peak power output and the quite high final drive ratio go with a flat torque curve that is characteristic of Vauxhall, and vindicated by above-average acceleration in top gear at speeds from 10 m.p.h. upwards. There has, incidentally, been a substantial improvement right through the range since the first Victor saloon was tested by *The Motor*. Inevitably, sporting driving habits are restricted by a three-speed gearbox with a maximum usable speed in second gear of about 50 m.p.h., and the engine although good at pulling is unresponsive to the accelerator, the more so on account of a rather vague linkage associated with the new organ-type pedal. A little surprisingly, this car with its obvious North American influence still retains a manual choke control (still superior on grounds of economy in town driving), and the handbook's claim that the engine will be ready to give its best within half a mile of starting from cold seems to be not far from the truth. (It is necessary to go rather further before much warmth comes through the interior heater.) British premium petrol, undiluted by even intermediate grades, proved necessary to avoid pinking when making full use of the engine's flexibility.

Restrictive in its choice of ratios, the gearbox nevertheless has a steering column gear change that is good by any standard and very good compared with some Vauxhalls in the past. The synchromesh—on all three forward gears—is of baulk-ring type which ensures perfectly silent engagement, but positive linkage makes it possible to snatch a change very quickly in emergency. The clutch is smooth and non-slipping but could be lighter.

The Victor's quality which is certain to please the enthusiast most is its handling. Again the fruit of painstaking research is evident in roadholding and steering which, if not in the sports-car class, stand at any rate half-way between those of sports cars and many run-of-the-mill family saloons. Using a conventional layout, without even

The engine has been made more accessible by increasing the bonnet opening. The bonnet is released by an external catch.

13

The tail exhibits less chromium and a neater bumper than hitherto. It is necessary to use the ignition key to open the boot.

such semi-sporting components as rack and pinion steering gear, the car has been endowed with steering that is both light and responsive, retaining plenty of feel for slippery road conditions but free from reaction. The anti-roll bar which is a part of the front suspension is clearly there more for its effect on steering characteristics than actually to limit the angle of heel, which is considerable. In spite of this rolling tendency the understeer is both moderate and consistent. Sticking to the road rather more effectively than an enthusiastic driver is able to stick to his seat without a firm hold on the wheel (although the separate seats are a big help), the Victor is not perhaps an ideal car with which to play tricks of the wiggle-woggle variety, but in compensation it plays no tricks back under normal conditions.

A glance at the technical specification is apt to cause slight apprehension amongst those who are accustomed to predict brake performance on the basis of friction lining area. At a mere 91.5 sq. in. per ton of unladen weight the Vauxhall should by these standards be suspect for mountain roads or fast driving. In practice an unusual design of composite brake drum, employing a cast-iron periphery on a light steel back plate, produces fade only after severe provocation, with fairly quick recovery and no increase in pedal travel through drum expansion. The hand-brake is of pull-out type under the facia, better than some in holding power.

Undoubtedly the stylists were given a fairly free hand with the original Victor, and their bolder creations have been to some extent toned down, as in the substitution of paint for chromium on the panel holding the heater controls and ashtray. Closer inspection shows that items like the speedometer, housed in a dial of unrelated shape, are more readable than many which conform to the circular tradition. Similarly the rather glossy row of switches turns out to be practical in operation. A two-position pull-out switch for the side and headlights is combined with a rheostat for the instrument panel illumination and a switch for the roof lamp, which has a lens throwing a bright narrow beam for reading as well as the normal diffused interior light. Alongside that is a combined two-speed windscreen wiper switch and button for the windscreen washers, and beside that an ignition and starter switch which allows the car to be left driveable if necessary in a garage with the boot locked and the key removed. Intelligent doubling-up of controls in this way makes for less confusion, especially in the dark. By contrast the tumbler switches for a pair of optional auxiliary driving lamps appear to have been an afterthought, hard to find and to reach, while there is a half-ring only for the horn.

The list of optional accessories is long—longer, perhaps, than one might expect on the most expensive model, which does not include in its purchase price such items as the interior heater, clock or even the useful parcel shelf supplementing a deep but narrow glove box. The luggage locker is unusually large for a 1½-litre saloon, openable only by key and possessing torsion bar springs for the lid which could be damaging to luggage if the boot were well filled.

A descriptive article on pages 167-169 gives details of some of the less apparent changes which have occurred in the Victor, some with the latest model and some gradually over the last two years. Many of the latter are associated with new methods of production and illustrate the meaning of the often unappreciated term "development." They confirm the findings of practical experience, that the latest of the Vauxhall line is a sound and sensible motorcar worth the attention of any four-seat-family motorist.

Specification

Engine
Cylinders	4
Bore	79.4 mm.
Stroke	76.2 mm.
Cubic capacity	1,507 c.c.
Piston area	30.7 sq. in.
Valves	pushrod o.h.v.
Compression ratio	7.8/1 (6.3 optional)
Carburetter	Zenith 34 VN downdraught
Fuel pump	AC mechanical
Ignition timing control	Centrifugal and vacuum
Oil filter	AC By-pass
Max power (gross)	54.8 b.h.p.
at	4,200 r.p.m.
Piston speed at max. b.h.p.	2,100 ft./min

Transmission
Clutch	Borg and Beck s.d.p. 7¼ in.
Top gear (s/m)	4.125
2nd gear (s/m)	6.75
1st gear (s/m)	13.14
Reverse	12.6
Propeller shaft	Hardy Spicer open
Final drive	Hypoid
Top gear m.p.h. at 1,000 r.p.m.	16.3
Top gear m.p.h. at 1,000 ft./min. piston speed	32.6

Chassis
Brakes	Lockheed hydraulic (2 l.s. front)
Brake drum internal diameter	8 in.
Friction lining area	92 sq. in.
Suspension:	
Front	Wishbones and coil springs
Rear	Semi-elliptic leaf
Shock absorbers:	
Front and rear	Vauxhall telescope
Steering gear	Burman recirculating ball
Tyres	5.60—13 tubeless

Coachwork and Equipment

Starting handle	No
Battery mounting	Beside engine
Jack	Scissor type
Jacking points	Two each side, under door sills

Standard tool kit: Wheelnut spanner, jack, sparking plug spanner, tommy bar, screwdriver, 2 O/E spanners, adjustable spanner, brake adjustment spanner.

Exterior lights: 2 head, 2 side/indicator, 2 tail/stop, 2 rear indicator, number plate.

Number of electrical fuses	2 with thermal interrupter for lights
Direction indicators	Flashing, self-cancelling (amber rear)
Windscreen wipers	2-speed electric, self-parking
Windscreen washers	Optional
Sun visors	Two

Instruments: Speedometer with non-trip, decimal distance recorder, water thermometer, fuel gauge.

Warning lights: Oil pressure, dynamo charge, headlamp main beam, indicators.

Locks:	
With ignition key	Ignition, boot, either front door
With other keys	None
Glove lockers	One
Map pockets	None
Parcel shelves	Optional
Ashtrays	One front, two rear
Cigar lighters	Optional
Interior lights	One in roof
Interior heater: Optional, combined fresh air and recirculating type with demister	
Car radio	Optional, Plessey V.R.V.

Extras available: Radio, heater, windscreen washers, wing mirrors, parcel shelf, fog lamps, exterior sun visor, roof rack, floor mats, reversing lights, seat covers, electric clock, etc.

Upholstery material	Leather
Floor covering	Carpet
Exterior colours standardized	Five single, four two-tone
Alternative body styles	Estate car

Maintenance

Sump	7.5 pints, S.A.E. 20
Gearbox	2.1 pints, S.A.E. 90
Rear axle	2.5 pints, S.A.E. 90
Steering gear lubricant	S.A.E. 90
Cooling system capacity	10¼ pints (2 drain taps)

Chassis lubrication: By grease gun every 1,000 miles to 17 points.

Ignition timing	9° b.t.d.c. static
Contact-breaker gap	0.019-0.021 in.
Sparking plug type	AC 44/5V
Sparking plug gap	0.028-0.030 in.

Valve timing: Inlet opens 19½° b.t.d.c.; inlet closes 60½° a.b.d.c.; exhaust opens 51½° b.b.d.c.; exhaust closes 28½° a.t.d.c.

Tappet clearances (hot):	
Inlet	0.013 in.
Exhaust	0.013 in.
Front wheel toe-in	0.125 in.
Camber angle	0° 38' laden
Castor angle	1° 30' laden
Steering swivel pin inclination	4°
Tyre pressures:	
Front	24 lb.
Rear	24 lb.
Brake fluid	Lockheed SAE 70 RZ
Battery type and capacity	Exide 6-XNF 7R, 43 amp. hr.

The Vauxhall Victor Super

Outmoded American styling features have been eliminated completely from the new Victor leaving just a pleasing and practical simplicity of line. Wing mirrors and fog lamps are extras.

A Family Car Which Sets High Standards of All-round Merit

AT the recent Earls Court Exhibition many people thought that, in the lower-price classes, the new Vauxhall stole the Show. Without being in any way unorthodox it seemed to offer just a little more in most directions than one could reasonably expect from a car at this price. Now that we have had the opportunity to test the Victor Super for more than 1,000 miles, we can say that its behaviour on the road fully matches the promise of its paper specification and in many ways exceeds it. It is, in fact, a car of remarkably wide appeal combining the qualities of space, comfort and silence, on which the week-end family motorist may place particular emphasis, with effortlessness and controllability—which will delight the expert who likes to work his car as near to the limit as prudence allows.

The new Victor is no mere face-lift of the previous model; wheelbase, track, length and width have all been increased and with them leg room, seat width and headroom, despite a reduction of 1½ in. in the overall height. Mounting the spare wheel upright in the wing space behind the offside rear wheel has helped to increase the useful boot volume. It was a considerable surprise to find that this roomier and much more attractive-looking car actually weighs 1¼ cwt. less than its predecessor, the Series 2 Victor we tested in March, 1959.

Of all the mechanical components the 1,508 c.c. four-cylinder engine has undergone the least apparent change although there have been numerous inconspicuous modifications to reduce weight and increase durability. New inlet and exhaust manifolds and a compression ratio of 8.1 instead of 7.8 have raised maximum power by 3% and torque by half this amount. A gentle driver could run quite happily on mixture grade fuel but full suppression of pinking throughout the speed range really demands the use of premium grade. Starting is excellent, whether hot or cold, and warming-up is quite rapid in spite of the elimination of the exhaust-heated hot spot in the new light-alloy inlet manifold.

Any potential improvements in top gear performance which might arise from higher torque and lower weight have been counterbalanced by a change in the final drive ratio from 4.125 to 3.9; fuel economy benefits appreciably from this and other modifications and steady speed consumption figures show improvements between 1½ and 4 m.p.g. in the range from 30 to 70 m.p.h. For the entire test the car returned an overall average of 26.4 m.p.g. and most private owners will have no difficulty in raising this figure by anything up to 6 m.p.g. With a very smooth and well-silenced engine, almost inaudible

The installation of the engine and accessories is unusually neat and accessible; the heater installation is all behind the bulkhead underneath the hinged scuttle flap and the air cleaner is much smaller than on many modern cars.

In Brief

Price (including 4-speed gearbox as tested) £547, plus purchase tax £251 18s. 11d. equals £798 18s. 11d.
Price with 3-speed gearbox (including purchase tax) .. .. £781 8s. 11d.
Capacity .. .. .. 1,508 c.c.
Unladen kerb weight .. 18¾ cwt.
Acceleration:
  20-40 m.p.h. in top gear 11.2 sec.
  0-50 m.p.h. through gears 14.7 sec.
Maximum top gear gradient 1 in 12.7
Maximum speed .. .. 76.2 m.p.h.
"Maximile" speed .. 75.5 m.p.h.
Touring fuel consumption 32.2 m.p.g.
Gearing: 17.3 m.p.h. in top gear at 1,000 r.p.m.; 34.6 m.p.h. at 1,000 ft./min. piston speed.

15

"THE MOTOR" ROAD TESTS

The Motor Road Test No. 39/61

Make: Vauxhall **Type:** Victor Super
Makers: Vauxhall Motors, Ltd., Luton, England

Test Data

World copyright reserved; no unauthorized reproduction in whole or in part.

CONDITIONS. Weather: Cool and dry with light wind. (Temperature 44°-50°F.; Barometer: 29.5 in. Hg.) Surface: Dry tarmacadam. Fuel: Premium grade pump petrol (approx. 97 Octane Rating by Research Method)

INSTRUMENTS
Speedometer at 30 m.p.h.	½% slow
Speedometer at 60 m.p.h.	accurate
Distance recorder	½% fast

WEIGHT
Kerb weight (unladen, but with oil, coolant and fuel for approx. 50 miles) .. 18¾ cwt.
Front/rear distribution of kerb weight .. 56/44
Weight laden as tested .. 22½ cwt.

MAXIMUM SPEEDS
Mean lap of banked circuit .. 76.2 m.p.h.
Best one-way quarter mile time equals 79.0 m.p.h.

"Maximile" speed. (Timed quarter mile after one mile accelerating from rest.)
Mean of opposite runs .. 75.5 m.p.h.
Best one-way time equals .. 77.6 m.p.h.

Speed in gears.
Max. speed in 3rd gear .. 70 m.p.h.
Max. speed in 2nd gear .. 45 m.p.h.
Max. speed in 1st gear .. 28 m.p.h.

FUEL CONSUMPTION
43 m.p.g. at constant 30 m.p.h. on level.
40 m.p.g. at constant 40 m.p.h. on level.
35½ m.p.g. at constant 50 m.p.h. on level.
30½ m.p.g. at constant 60 m.p.h. on level.
25½ m.p.g. at constant 70 m.p.h. on level.

Overall Fuel Consumption for 909 miles, 34½ gallons, equals 26.4 m.p.g. (10.7 litres/100 km.)

Touring Fuel Consumption (m.p.g. at steady speed midway between 30 m.p.h. and maximum, less 5% allowance for acceleration). 32.2 m.p.g.
Fuel tank capacity (maker's figure) 10 gallons.

STEERING
Turning circle between kerbs
Left .. 31¼ feet
Right .. 31¼ feet
Turns of steering wheel from lock to lock 3⅓

BRAKES from 30 m.p.h.
1.00 g retardation (equivalent to 30 ft. stopping distance) with 80 lb. pedal pressure.
0.95 g retardation (equivalent to 31½ ft. stopping distance) with 75 lb. pedal pressure.
0.76 g retardation (equivalent to 39½ ft. stopping distance) with 50 lb. pedal pressure.
0.32 g retardation (equivalent to 94 ft. stopping distance) with 25 lb. pedal pressure.

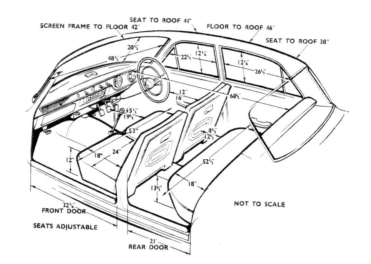

ACCELERATION TIMES from standstill.
0-30 m.p.h.	5.8 sec.
0-40 m.p.h.	9.1 sec.
0-50 m.p.h.	14.7 sec.
0-60 m.p.h.	22.6 sec.
0-70 m.p.h.	37.7 sec.
Standing quarter mile	22.1 sec.

ACCELERATION TIMES on upper ratios
	Top Gear	Third Gear
10-30 m.p.h.	11.7 sec.	7.7 sec.
20-40 m.p.h.	11.2 sec.	7.4 sec.
30-50 m.p.h.	12.5 sec.	8.9 sec.
40-60 m.p.h.	17.5 sec.	13.4 sec.
50-70 m.p.h.	25.6 sec.	—

HILL CLIMBING at sustained steady speeds.
Max. gradient on top gear .. 1 in 12.7 (Tapley 175 lb./ton)
Max. gradient on 3rd gear .. 1 in 8.6 (Tapley 260 lb./ton)
Max. gradient on 2nd gear .. 1 in 5.2 (Tapley 425 lb./ton)

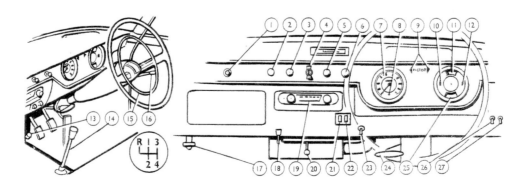

1, Glove locker catch. 2, Blank for cigar lighter. 3, Choke. 4, Ignition/starter. 5, Wipers and windscreen washers control. 6, Lights, panel and interior lamp switch. 7, Speedometer. 8, Main beam warning light. 9, Direction indicator warning light. 10, Dynamo charge warning light. 11, Fuel gauge. 12, Oil pressure warning light. 13, Dip switch. 14, Gear lever. 15, Horn ring. 16, Direction indicator warning light. 17, Bonnet release. 18, Scuttle ventilator. 19, Radio. 20, Fresh air control. 21, Demister. 22, Heat control. 23, Heater fan switch. 24, Hand brake. 25, Water temperature gauge. 26, Near side fog lamp switch. 27, Off side fog lamp switch.

16

The Vauxhall Victor Super

at tickover and never conspicuous at any speed, this high top gear gives very quiet effortless motoring at any speed up to the 76 m.p.h. maximum which we held for mile after mile on a motorway. Naturally, this easy cruising involves some small sacrifice in top gear acceleration and hill climbing but few drivers will feel this to be much of a hardship if they elect to have the superb 4-speed all-synchromesh gearbox with which our test car was fitted and which is offered (at extra cost) as an alternative to the standard 3-speed unit.

It is certainly not beyond criticism. The intermediate gears are not silent although the noise they make is not unpleasant, and the floor-mounted remote control has a rather springy linkage which promotes some vagueness of feel. A long fore and aft travel together with a big movement across the gate puts reverse gear at the limit of comfortable reach when the driving seat is pushed right back (as it may be for a driver of over 5 ft. 9 in.) and the reverse catch is not very definite. But such is the charm of this gearbox that after a little use even the disadvantages seem to be advantages. Long travel goes with extreme lightness and smoothness so that only finger-tip pressure is needed for the highly effective synchronizing mechanism, and the rather springy mechanical connections seem to isolate the lever most effectively from the usual engine noise and vibration. Third gear gives an entirely unflurried 60 m.p.h. with a more obtrusive 10 m.p.h. in hand and second is not just a traffic ratio but is high enough to be really useful in minor-road motoring. A 28 m.p.h. first with excellent synchromesh ceases to be just the usual emergency starting gear and becomes surprisingly useful in town; it proved low enough to restart on a 1 in 4 gradient but not on 1 in 3, both engine torque and clutch capacity being inadequate for the latter. The pull-out handbrake held quite easily on these gradients but, except for a short driver with the seat well forward, was just a little too far away to be really convenient.

In the "off" positions, brake and accelerator pedals were fairly close together and in the same plane giving very rapid transfer of the right foot from one to the other and also an ideal relationship for "heel and toe" braking and gearchanging. A year or two ago a footbrake giving 1% retardation for every pound of force exerted on it was considered quite light; now many cars need much less effort than this, the Victor giving nearer 1½% per lb. force but still retaining a very satisfactory sensitivity and progressiveness. Relatively small cast-iron brake drums (8 in. dia.) which are unusually rigid seem very difficult indeed to fade in this country.

There is no doubt that this Vauxhall gives a very soft and extremely comfortable pitch-free ride in both front and back seats over most kinds of surfaces. At low speeds the front suspension is a little obtrusive when passing over sharp bumps and potholes, transmitting some tremor and shock through the structure and producing steering column vibration on washboard surfaces. At higher speeds all this seems to smooth away completely leaving nothing worse than a little road rumble on some surfaces.

With only the driver on board the live back axle will sometimes hop a little on bumps but this tendency diminishes with increasing load and the behaviour is certainly above average for this kind of rear suspension. Understeer is the basic cornering characteristic and even when the car is thrown about in the most carefree fashion it never does anything sudden or unpredictable on wet roads or dry. On corners there is very little tyre squeal but quite a lot of roll which seems to have little effect on the accuracy of the light steering. The latter gives no initial impression of being unusually positive but in a thoroughly unobtrusive way it directs the car with great accuracy to where the driver wants it on straight roads and bends alike. It gives very little kick back but plenty of feel, and the smoothness it shares with most of the other controls should remain since the steering swivels have been redesigned to need lubrication only at intervals of 12,000 miles. The driver feels very much at ease and in command, and this makes the Victor a restful car to drive for long periods.

The ordinary and Super Victors are fitted with a bench front seat but the individual front seats which are standard on the de luxe model are available on the cheaper versions at an extra cost of less than £15. They were fitted to the

Although the Victor is quite low it is a very easy car to enter and leave because of wide front doors and a limited amount of screen wrap-round. Instruments are well below the normal line of sight and could with advantage face upwards more.

The road test car was fitted with the diagonal belt safety harness which is offered as a Vauxhall accessory. The rear door handles are inoperative when the locking buttons are depressed, a child-proofing feature.

The Vauxhall Victor Super

Available only in four door form, the body is very carefully protected against rust. The underbody panel and the under sides of the wings are sealed with a bituminous plastic coat not less than 1/16 in. thick for noise reduction as well as corrosion resistance.

road test car and proved well shaped and quite comfortable for fairly long distances in spite of quite hard upholstery. Lateral support was better than the shape of the backrest suggested, partly because of the good friction properties of the Vynide covering and partly because the occupants can sit in a high and upright position with the feet braced well apart. Most passengers might prefer to recline a little more but the driver feels properly placed with a very good view of the road over a sloping bonnet and little interference with his all round vision from thin screen pillars. The steering wheel position seemed to please different-sized drivers with varying tastes but some found the arm rest fixed to the front door to be rather a nuisance. The back seat provides adequate leg room and width for three quite tall people but the outer ones tend to be pushed towards the centre by a back rest which curves round at the ends to meet the body sides. No central arm rest is fitted.

A large ventilator is fitted to the scuttle just forward of the centre of the windscreen with a lever projecting below the facia to control its opening. When the optional heater is fitted the incoming fresh air from this vent can be raised to a temperature which is controlled thermostatically and remains constant irrespective of the actual quantity of air flow. On the test car this was rather spoiled by a tendency for the temperature control lever to work towards the "cold" position and by a setting which was over-sensitive, most of the effective adjustment being concentrated into one end of its range of movement. At low speeds air flow can be boosted by a two-speed fan which has a separate control switch but is also selected automatically when the air control lever is set to give maximum demisting.

If the optional safety harness is worn, the driver finds these heater controls difficult to reach and the same is true of the optional fog light switches fitted under the right-hand side of the dashboard. Not everyone likes the rather loose stainless steel trimming of the facia board but the control knobs work positively and the instrument dials are as clear as they are uninformative. A remarkably accurate speedometer is calibrated only at 10 m.p.h. intervals, the fuel gauge has only a single dot (half way?) between empty and full and the water thermometer says only H and C with no indication of a normal running range. The facia contains a glove locker of adequate size but there are no other map pockets or parcel shelves in the front compartment although a shelf is available for another 13s. 6d.

This new Victor is a striking example of how very much higher the family car designers are now setting their sights. In springing, accommodation and refinement it can live with the luxury car of only a few years ago; in ease and certainty of handling it is very much superior.

Specification

Engine

Cylinders	4
Bore	79.4 mm
Stroke	76.2 mm.
Cubic capacity	1,508 c.c.
Piston area	30.7 sq. in.
Valves	o.h.v. (pushrods)
Compression ratio	8.1/1
Carburetter	Zenith 34VN downdraught
Fuel pump	AC mechanical
Ignition timing control	Centrifugal and vacuum
Oil filter	AC by-pass
Max. power (net)	49.5 b.h.p. (56.3 gross) at 4,600 r.p.m.
Piston speed at max. b.h.p.	2,300 ft./min.

Transmission

Clutch	Borg & Beck $7\frac{1}{4}$ in. s.d.p.
Top gear (s/m)	3.9
3rd gear (s/m)	5.28
2nd gear (s/m)	8.31
1st gear (s/m)	12.83
Reverse	11.89
Propeller shaft	Single-piece open
Final drive	10/39 Hypoid bevel
Top gear m.p.h. at 1,000 r.p.m.	17.3
Top gear m.p.h. at 1,000 ft./min. piston speed	34.6

Chassis

Brakes	Lockheed hydraulic (2 l.s. at front)
Brake dimensions	8 in. dia. × $1^{7}/_{16}$ in. wide
Friction areas	92 sq. in. of lining working on 150.6 sq. in. rubbed area of drums.
Suspension:	
Front	Independent by coil springs, transverse wishbones and anti-roll torsion bar.
Rear	Rigid axle and $\frac{1}{2}$-elliptic leaf springs.
Shock Absorbers	Telescopic
Steering gear	Burman recirculating ball
Tyres	5.60-13 tubeless 4-ply

Coachwork and Equipment

Starting handle	None
Battery mounting	Alongside engine on right
Jack	Screwed pedestal type
Jacking points	2 each side underneath body
Standard tool kit	Jack, jack handle and wheel-nut spanner.
Exterior lights	2 headlamps 2 sidelamps, 2 stop/tail lamps, rear number plate lamp.
Number electrical fuses	4 (also thermal circuit-breaker in lighting switch).
Direction indicators	Self-cancelling flashers
Windscreen wipers	Electrical twin-blade, self-parking.
Windscreen washers	Optional extra (Trico-suction type.
Sun visors	Two, universally pivoted
Instruments	Speedometer with decimal total distance recorder, fuel contents gauge, coolant thermometer.
Warning lights	Dynamo charge, oil pressure, headlamp main beam, turn indicators.
Locks: With ignition key	Ignition/starter switch (this can be left free for use without key), either front door, boot.
With other keys	None
Glove lockers	One on facia, with lid
Map pockets	None
Parcel shelves	None (shelf for mounting below facia optional as extra).
Ashtrays	One on facia, 2 behind front seats
Cigar lighters	Socket for optional extra provided on facia
Interior lights	One in roof, with courtesy and manual switches
Interior heater	Optional extra fresh-air heater and screen demister
Car radio	Optional extra
Extras available	4-speed gearbox, individual front seats, heater, screen washers, radio, cigar lighter, foglamps, reversing lamp.
Upholstery material	Vynide
Floor covering	Carpet
Exterior colours standardized	14 (with 3 upholstery colours).
Alternate body styles	Standard and de Luxe versions of same body and Estate Car.

Maintenance

Sump	$7\frac{1}{2}$ pints, S.A.E. 20W for temperate summer and winter
Gearbox	2 pints, S.A.E. 90 gear oil
Rear axle	$2\frac{1}{2}$ pints, S.A.E. 90 hypoid gear oil
Steering gear lubricant	S.A.E. 90 gear oil
Cooling system capacity	$11\frac{3}{4}$ pints plus $1\frac{1}{2}$ pints in heater (2 drain taps)
Chassis lubrication	By grease gun (graphited grease) every 12,000 miles to 4 points
Ignition timing	9° before t.d.c. static
Contact-breaker gap	0.019-0.021 in.
Sparking plug type	AC 14 mm. type 44/5V
Sparking plug gap	0.0528-0.032 in.
Valve timing	Inlet opens 19.6° before t.d.c. and closes 60.6° after b.d.c.; exhaust opens 51.6° before b.d.c. and closes 28.6° after t.d.c.
Tappet clearances (hot)	Inlet and exhaust 0.013 in.
Front wheel toe-in	$\frac{1}{8}$ in. to $^{5}/_{32}$ in.
Camber angle	$\frac{1}{4}$° to $1\frac{1}{4}$°
Castor angle	1° to $2\frac{1}{2}$°
Steering swivel pin inclination	5° to 6°
Tyre pressures	Front 24 lb. Rear 24 lb.
Brake and clutch fluid	Lockheed Super Heavy Duty (S.A.E. Spec. 70.R.3)
Battery type and capacity	12 volt 38 amp. hr. (Exide 6VTMZ-9L or Lucas BHN-9A)

Vauxhall VX Four-Ninety

Too many carburetters?

FROM one point of view, it really seems as if the Vauxhall VX 4/90 has one carburetter too many. With two carburetters on its 1,508 c.c. engine it is a delightful and far from extravagant car, but twin carburetters are closely associated in many minds with sports car characteristics whereas this is essentially a fast touring model. Its exclusive light-alloy cylinder head lets the VX 4/90 engine develop a lot more power than the Victor engine of equal size, adding about 12 m.p.h. to the maximum speed of a four-door saloon, and there are such features as disc front brakes and stiffened suspension to let good use be made of this extra power. In its well-balanced character however, this Vauxhall remains a 1½-litre family or business car of all-round excellence, well behaved and very fully equipped as well as boasting above-average performance —but it is not a sports car. The twin carburetters could do this model a double disservice if they attracted a few buyers who really wanted something more fiercely sporting, and frightened off the much more numerous motorists who would be delighted by its fast-touring qualities.

Velvet gloved

FLAT-OUT around a banked test track with the accelerator pedal kept on the floorboards for about a dozen miles, the VX 4/90 (which came to us with just under 3,000 miles on its distance recorder) showed lap speeds of between 88 and 89 m.p.h., the speed going up towards 95 m.p.h. on the downwind side of the circuit and dropping below 85 m.p.h. against the wind. Each lap was a tiny fraction faster than its predecessor, suggesting that whereas sustained speed tires some cars, this high-geared model was merely finishing its running-in process.

With its 88½ m.p.h. maximum speed, this is not the fastest

DISTINGUISHED from other 1,508 c.c. Vauxhalls by a coloured flash on the body sides, a distinctive radiator grille of reduced depth and vertical stop lamps, the VX 4/90 is the fastest and most fully equipped model in a four-car series.

In Brief

Price £674 plus purchase ta £253 15s. 3d. equals £927 15s. 3d
Capacity .. .. 1,508 c.c
Unladen kerb weight 19½ cw
Acceleration:
  20-40 m.p.h. in top gear 11.7 sec
  0-50 m.p.h. through gears
    11.9 sec
Maximum top-gear gradient
    1 in 11.
Maximum speed .. 88.4 m.p.h
"Maximile" speed .. 84.6 m.p.h
Touring fuel consumption
    30 m.p.g
Gearing: 17.8 m.p.h. in top gear a 1,000 r.p.m.

TRADITIONAL in style, the interior of a four-door saloon body is furnished entirely in modern synthetic materials.

Vauxhall VX Four-Ninety

car in its class, but a 3.9 axle ratio means that at this pace the engine has not quite reached peak r.p.m., and a driver need have little compunction about making regular use of the available speed. The high axle ratio gives the car a very effortless stride, and at any cruising speed this high-compression Vauxhall is actually more economical of fuel than a normal Victor. Extra torque almost offsets the gearing-up effect of larger-diameter wheels so far as top gear acceleration at speeds below 30 m.p.h. is concerned, and the VX 4/90 keeps on pulling hard over a much extended speed range so that at 60 m.p.h. it has 50% better top gear pulling power than the Victor. Fast-idle linkages on the choke mechanism of our test car seemed maladjusted for cold starting, but once started the engine was exceptionally quick in settling down to pull normally without help from the choke.

High gearing has not prevented this car having the docility expected of a family saloon, and it will pull away from about 15 m.p.h. in top gear without hesitancy or transmission snatch although individual power impulses from the 4-cylinder engine are felt until the speed rises above 25 m.p.h. The choice of a high axle ratio does however make one especially appreciative of a delightful four-speed gearbox which has synchromesh on all ratios.

For the keen driver, the gearbox offers quick changes controlled by a central floor-mounted lever: operating the gears through an under-floor linkage, the lever is not altogether positive in feel, but has the merit of providing some insulation from the high-frequency engine vibration that afflicts many gear lever knobs. One can hold 3rd gear up to more than 70 m.p.h. when overtaking other traffic without the r.p.m. indicator needle reaching its red sector. The lower two gears also are genuinely meant to be used when the liveliest possible getaway from low speeds is required, bottom being virtually a 30 m.p.h. ratio, only just low enough to re-start a reasonable load on a 1 in 4 hill. It is a vivid demonstration of truly effective synchromesh to go up through the gears from bottom to top without touching the clutch, making each successive change silently by releasing the accelerator while two-finger pressure is applied to the gear lever, which will move into neutral, check momentarily as the engine speed drops and then move into the next gear position at the precise instant when the speeds of the dog-clutch halves are synchronized.

Body shaping that keeps wind noise down to a moderate level complements high gearing to make this an unfussy car at fairly high cruising speeds. Opening the front ventilator panels does not bring much extra sound of rushing air. Isolation of road noise from the passengers has been less successful, for while bumps are not heard a good deal of rumble is evident in the front during moderate speed driving on many non-skid road surfaces, and in fast motorway driving road rumble from the rear of the body is a nuisance. One would like to see improvement in the isolation of road noise, but the overall impression which this car leaves with most people is of very reasonable interior quietness in top gear and of only moderate engine noise during hard acceleration through the gears.

Interior orthodoxy

BODY furnishing in the VX 4/90 achieves a traditional effect from non-traditional materials. Some painted metal panels, areas of nicely grained mock woodwork, soft imitation leather upholstery and a washable plastic roof lining are the raw materials, yet this carpeted interior gives very much the atmosphere of a traditional sports saloon. Individual front seats, the short and well-placed central gear lever and pull-up handbrake, a full set of instruments with circular black dials, and map pockets in the doors are details contributing to a pleasant atmosphere.

As usual, one finds a range of driving seat adjustment insufficient to make a 6-ft. tall man comfortable, a steering wheel position which is convenient for use proving to impede entry to the driving seat for the long-legged. Some people found the driving seat comfortable, others felt the need for extra small-of-the-back support; but most front seat passengers thought that more sideways support than the backrest provided would have made fast travel down winding roads less tiring. With the limited scope for a driver to stretch his legs there is, naturally enough, always room for two quite big men in the back, where a folding armrest can divide the comfortably shaped seat and where three abreast seating is not impossibly crowded.

Fitted as standard, the interior heater draws fresh air from a scuttle-top intake. A small temperature-regulating lever mounted inconspicuously beneath the facia is rather sensitive to adjust, but as it sets a thermostat a pleasantly consistent degree of warmth is maintained once the preferred setting has been found. A slight stuffiness can result because foot-warming has to be accompanied by some delivery of warm air on to the windscreen interior. Very effective electrical windscreen wipers cover overlapping arcs, but a quieter motor would be an improvement; the twist-switch for the wipers also controls a suction-type screen washer when it is pulled outwards. All four doors of the body have a form of child-protecting safety lock, in that when a locking button is pressed the interior handle (as well as the exterior handle) becomes inoperative until the button is pulled up again.

CIRCULAR DIALS with white figures on black faces are used on the grained facia panel. A horn ring, and central remote control for an all-synchromesh four-speed gearbox are other details in the photograph below.

LOW LOADING luggage locker which the VX 4/90 shares with Vauxhall Victors is shown below. The spare wheel is completely recessed into one rear wing.

SPACIOUSNESS is a feature of the under-bonnet layout. A vacuum servo for the disc-and-drum braking system is behind the battery, and a windscreen washer reservoir to the right of two downdraught carburetters.

In the tail of the body, a luggage locker of generous size has a virtually flat floor, and no sill impedes easy loading of heavy trunks. The spare wheel stands up at one side of the locker, and below the floor is a 10-gallon tank which gives a reasonably generous range. Map pockets, a glove box, a shelf below the rear window and an extra parcel shelf on the nearside of the facia panel provide better accommodation for personal belongings than in most other recent Vauxhalls.

Straight and Level

STIFFER springs and a more powerful anti-roll torsion bar are used on the VX 4/90 than on other Victor models, yet this car seems "just right" rather than taut in its riding characteristics. There is a versatile ability to cope inconspicuously with extremely varied sorts of going; the springs are soft enough to take the sting out of bad bumps yet well enough controlled not to accentuate switchbacks. Sharp ridges or "washboard" corrugations cause shake of the structure and some steering reaction, but are rarely encountered in Britain where this is a comfortably sprung car. Rear seat riding is exceptionally good.

Roll on corners is sensibly diminished in comparison with more softly sprung Victors, but not by any means eliminated, and if normal inflation pressures are used it remains fairly easy to provoke front tyre scuffling or squeal on corners. One could not ask that this model should be safer on corners than the other Victor models, which themselves never seem to put a foot wrong, but it has the same consistent behaviour unmarred by any nasty surprises. Driven normally it understeers, whereas when cornered very hard it begins to "hang its tail out" (on wet surfaces, this effect seemed to begin a little earlier than is usual with modern "cling rubber" tyres) but the transition is so gradual that it merely warns the driver that he is approaching the danger limit.

Although there is a slight amount of flexibility to insulate the driver's hands against road shock, this Vauxhall's steering feels beautifully precise and frictionless. Camber changes and wind gusts are felt, yet keeping a straight course in any but freakish conditions seems to involve no more than slight instinctive steering action, rather than the conscious correction of wander which makes some cars tiring to drive.

Individual front seats have left room in this Vauxhall model for a central pull-up handbrake, which can just hold the car on a 1 in 3 test hill and meets normal requirements very easily indeed. Disc-type front brakes and a vacuum servo to assist their application are another VX 4/90 feature, there being instant and powerful response to quite modest pedal effort at traffic speeds and a simulated emergency stop from 90 m.p.h. showed it to be almost too easy to keep the wheels on the locking point. The pad material which gives this "bite" in normal motoring is perhaps less hard than those used in some other disc-brake systems, and there was a very evident reduction in braking power (mostly a loss of front braking effect) after half a dozen test stops from 60 m.p.h. had been made in quick succession. Once more, it must be said that this is not a sports car, and the right buyer will enjoy the instant braking response without ever approaching the disc temperature at which some fade occurs.

It is as a very good all-rounder that this Vauxhall VX 4/90 makes a strong appeal. Above-average performance without very high running costs, reassuringly safe handling qualities in conjunction with comfortable riding, and a neat looking, well-furnished body of a popular size add up to extremely pleasant motoring for a price below £930.

Coachwork and Equipment

Starting handle ... ... None
Battery mounting ... Alongside engine on right
Jack ... ... Screw pillar type
Jacking points ... 2 external sockets under each side of body
Standard tool kit: Jack and handle, tool bag containing pliers, adjustable spanner, 2 double-ended open-jaw spanners, sparking plug spanner and tommy bar, wheel nut spanner, normal and Phillips screwdrivers.
Exterior lights: 2 headlamps, 2 sidelamps, 2 stop/tail lamps, rear number plate lamp.
Number of electrical fuses: 4 fuses, 1 thermal circuit breaker in lighting switch.
Direction indicators ... Self-cancelling amber flashers
Windscreen wipers ... Twin-blade electrical, self-parking
Windscreen washers ... ... Suction type
Sun visors... ... ... Two, universally pivoted
Instruments: Speedometer with total and decimal trip distance recorders, r.p.m. indicator, fuel contents gauge, oil pressure gauge, ammeter, coolant thermometer.
Warning lights ... Dynamo charge, headlamp main beam, turn indicators
Locks:
With ignition key: Ignition/starter switch (can be left unlocked if desired), either front door, luggage locker.
With other keys: None.
Glove lockers ... ... One on facia, with lid
Map pockets ... Two inside front doors
Parcel shelves ... One on nearside of facia, one behind rear seat
Ashtrays ... One on facia, one in each rear door
Cigar lighters ... Provision on facia for fitting as optional extra
Interior lights: One in roof, with switch on facia and courtesy switches on front doors.
Interior heater ... Fresh-air heater and screen de-mister
Car radio ... ... Optional extra
Extras available: Radio, exterior mirrors, foglamps, radiator blind, loose mats, anti-mist panel for rear window, exterior sun visor, towing attachment, roof rack, cigar lighter, petrol tank lock, etc.
Upholstery material ... ... Imitation leather
Floor covering ... ... Carpet
Exterior colours standardized ... 9, with 4 interior colours
Alternative body styles: None. (Victor standard, Super, de Luxe and Estate Car are lower-performance versions of same 4-door body.)

Maintenance

Sump ... 7½ pints, S.A.E. 20W (or multi-grade) summer and winter
Gearbox ... ... 2.1 pints, S.A.E. 90
Rear axle ... 2.5 pints, S.A.E. 90 hypoid oil
Steering gear lubricant ... ... S.A.E. 90 oil
Cooling system capacity ... 13 pints (2 drain taps)
Chassis lubrication: By grease gun (special long-life grease) every 12,000 miles to 4 points.
Ignition timing ... ... 9° before t.d.c. static
Contact breaker gap ... ... 0.019-0.021 in.
Sparking plug type ... 14 mm. AC type 44XL
Sparking plug gap ... ... 0.028-0.032 in.
Valve timing:
Inlet opens 29.6° before t.d.c. and closes 76.1° a.b.d.c.
Exhaust opens 71.6° before b.d.c. and closes 34.1° a.t.d.c.
Tappet clearances (hot) Inlet and exhaust 0.013 in.
Front wheel toe-in ... ... ⅛ in. to 5/32 in.
Camber angle ... ... ¼° to 1¼°
Castor angle ... ... 1° to 2¼°
Steering swivel pin inclination... ... 5° to 6°
Tyre pressures ... ... Front and rear 26 lb.
Brake fluid ... Lockheed Super Heavy Duty (S.A.E. Spec. 70.R.3)
Battery ... 12 volt, 38 amp. hr., Exide 6VTMZ-9L or Lucas BHW9A

21

Belying its appearance, the estate car is in fact no longer than the Victor saloons. A considerable area of glass and the downward slope of the short bonnet make for excellent visibility. The fuel filler is concealed behind a hinged flap near the tail, and a lock for this is listed as an extra

VAUXHALL VICTOR ESTATE CAR

AT this time many British products are being judged in relation to a state of affairs which does not yet exist for them—the Common Market—which may be years away. The motor industry, until recently the largest exporter of all, is naturally under especially keen surveillance. When a new car is pitched into the maelstrom, it has to be better than good enough; to become a worth-while international project it should be aimed higher than all its Continental rivals.

From the moment of its first presentation in September, 1961, the new Vauxhall Victor has aroused very wide interest because of its graceful, unostentatious appearance, its useful size and low price. A large range of optional equipment, including a four-speed gearbox and separate front seats, gives the prospective owner the opportunity to have it the way it suits him best.

In this case the estate version was tested; it is a particularly elegant and well-planned vehicle, with four side doors and a single loading gate hinged at roof level. As the tail of the vehicle has a pronounced slope these hinges are well forward, and consequently the gate does not swing out far beyond the bumper as it is raised. It is, of course, counterbalanced. The large rear window is fixed, as are the side windows nearest to it.

With the back seat set up normally, the platform length behind it is 3ft 7in. long. As the seat squab is held in place only by rubber buttons sprung into sockets, it would be unwise to carry a weighty load behind it without having this modified to give some positive security against an abrupt stop. With the seat folded down, however, when the platform becomes 5ft 5in. long, the under-surface of the cushion becomes a positive vertical "wall." The loading platform is covered with felt carpeting faced with thick plastic, secured by chrome rubbing strips, and the spare wheel is tucked away vertically behind the off-side rear wheel arch. Jack and tools are stowed beneath the rear-seat cushion. Maximum recommended load is 1,000lb (9 cwt) including driver and passengers; with a driver and one passenger approximately 700lb (6¼ cwt) can still be carried.

In standard form the estate car costs £862, including U.K. purchase tax. The car tested was fitted with a number of extras, of which the most important were a fresh air heater, the four-speed gearbox with floor change and individual front seats, these three bringing the cost up to £909. Seat trim of this model is in a tough Vynide with a silvery sheen. The seats are firmly upholstered, quite well-shaped and comfortable, although a little more curvature of the backrests would be welcomed by those who like to make good use of the car's fast cornering abilities.

From the driving seat everything feels correct from the start. One sits fairly upright, commanding an excellent view all round, and the steering wheel is set where it impedes neither movement beneath it nor vision above it. It is conveniently raked from the vertical without any appreciable sideways offset, and has a comfortable rim with finger grips. The brake and clutch pedals have big, square pads and hence spread the operating load over a larger area of the foot than is usual. Their angles of attack are as they should be, which is so rarely the case with pendant pedals. The organ-type accelerator, however, swings

With the back seat lowered the platform length is 5ft 5in., but there is—probably wisely—no provision for overhanging loads

through much too wide an angle between closed and full throttle positions, keeping the ankle joint very busy.

Very conveniently placed are the central gear lever and parking brake T-handle, which is to the left of the steering column. Deeply recessed and set low relative to the driver's eyes, the instrument dials offer rather vague indications of speed, fuel level and water temperature, having few gradations. Minor controls are down to the practical minimum, and include four in the middle of the facia. These are, from left to right, the choke, the combined ignition and starter switch (which can be set to function without the key); then the wiper switch, which is also pulled to operate the quick-response vacuum screenwash; and, lastly, the lighting switch. This controls a rheostat for the instruments and the roof lamp as well as the driving lamps. By shifting the lighting switch to the right of the instruments any possibility of confusion with the wiper switch in an emergency would be avoided.

The several heater controls are soon learned. Particularly useful is a quick-action lever by which a powerful boost can be directed instantly at the screen. For normal heating there is a booster with a two-way switch when required, and the fresh air inlet on the scuttle is adjustable. A commendable Vauxhall feature for some time past has been thermostatic control of interior heat, which keeps the temperature constant regardless of car speed and the varying amount of air entering it.

The screen has no sharp curvature and the single-speed wipers clear it effectively at any speed. Flexible padded sun visors are fitted; their "free" ends are normally gripped in rubber jaws and they can be released and swung round when required. There is a small locker in the facia with push-button release above it, a lock for this costing a few shillings extra. There are no door pockets, however, nor any other provision for stowing maps, dusters and oddments.

No fundamental changes were made to the Victor's engine when the car was so completely transformed in other respects, for the good reason that it is an admirable unit providing adequate performance with less fuss and commotion than most other 1½-litres. It starts easily, warms quickly and runs very sweetly, no matter how hard it is pressed.

The estate car has lower final drive gearing than the saloon—4.13 as compared with 3.9 to 1—this representing 16 m.p.h. per 1,000 engine r.p.m. Thus, at the mean maximum of 77 m.p.h. the engine turns at around 4,800 r.p.m., or about 200 r.p.m. above peak power revs. Yet the Victor will glide along motorways at literally its maximum speed with extraordinary ease, quietness and smoothness. Indeed, it achieves this in the manner of a much higher-geared car. It is also a tractable unit which will pull smoothly down to about 1,000 r.p.m., although the superb four-speed gearbox removes any incentive to slogging at low revs.

This new box, with faultless synchromesh on all gears,

Left: Extending right up to the roof, where it is hinged, the loading door contains a deep window. Rear lamp and reflector clusters are small and neat, and a reversing lamp is a listed extra. Right: The Victor has an excellent driving position and particularly large, well-placed brake and clutch pedals. The two instrument dials are set rather low beneath the padded coaming. Rubber matting covers the floor

has a light movement and a narrow gate, and is so enjoyable to use that, even were an automatic transmission available for the Victor, surely few owners would choose to have it. For ordinary use the ratios are intelligently spaced, peaking in first at 26 m.p.h., in second at 40 and in third at 65, these figures being at approximately 5,500 r.p.m.

When it comes to climbing very steep hills, however, first is not quite low enough; thus with two up and no load the car cannot restart on 1-in-3, although the parking brake holds it squarely on this gradient. With its full load of 1,000lb it cannot restart on 1-in-4. Hence for hilly terrains its load-carrying capacity could only be used to the full were a lower overall gearing fitted. Among the figures in the

Four people with a mountain of luggage could travel far and comfortably in this estate car. There are cutaways for the rear passengers' feet in the front squabs. A small armrest is attached to each door, but there is no folding centre rest for the back seat. Both front doors have external locks

Vauxhall Victor Estate Car...

performance data panel, those in brackets indicate how the Vauxhall's accelerative powers are affected by a full load. It will be seen that from zero to 50 m.p.h. occupies only 4·3sec longer than in the normal testing condition of two up.

On the test car the transmission was very quiet, the rear axle making no audible whine. The overall fuel consumption for 1,095 miles, including all testing, was 25·9 m.p.g. This could be regarded as a little heavier than most private owners would achieve, and 30 m.p.g. should be within reach over long mileages if the car is not driven too hard. A 10-gallon tank thus provides a practical touring range of around 220 miles. Following the test, only one pint of oil was required to top the sump up to "full" on the dipstick.

For some years Vauxhalls have been among the better-sprung cars, and the new Victor, with its longer wheelbase and wider track than its predecessor's, rides with real comfort and stability in most conditions. Two unwanted legacies from the earlier car remain. While the suspension is of relatively low rate and quite soft, there is a certain harshness about the ride at low speeds which might lead one to expect excessive tyre pressures, or tyres with rather stiff walls. In fact, the Michelins fitted have very flexible walls, and the same phenomenon has been experienced in other new Victors with different makes of tyre.

Allied to this, a lot of road rumble comes up through the structure, particularly over certain coarse tarmac surfaces, and such obstacles as potholes and cats' eyes, although scarcely felt, offend the ear. The integral body structure is, in fact, rather "live," for on indifferent surfaces minor creaks and rattles can be heard which suggest the need for greater structural rigidity—in particular, the floor vibrates. On the special M.I.R.A. test surfaces the Vauxhall performed quite adequately. Over the very rough Belgian pavé the suspension did not reach its bump stops, although there was some float and the need for steering corrections at 40 m.p.h.

On wet or dry roads the car can be cornered surprisingly fast without sliding, and the front anti-roll bar keeps its body sway within very moderate limits. Only on a bumpy surface is there any tendency to rear axle hop, and the car is not plagued with tyre squeal.

Like all Vauxhalls it has very light steering which is without lost motion and quite precise. This enables one to place the car where one wishes, and no concentration is required to hold the car accurately on course, even in a fair cross wind. A little road vibration is felt sometimes at the steering wheel but otherwise it is free from noticeable reactions. Until the car is heavily laden its steering behaviour on corners is practically neutral, with a trace of understeer; as might be expected, this becomes an oversteer and results in some tail swing when this end of the car is full to capacity.

Perfectly ordinary drum brakes are fitted, which give powerful and sensitive response to quite moderate pressures. In fact, after a spell of driving cars with disc brakes one might well suspect the Vauxhall of having a servo motor. A highest stopping efficiency of 0·84g is quite reasonable; when attempts were made to improve upon this figure there was apparently some suspension wind-up which brought about some rather noisy reactions beneath the car.

There are several points about the Vauxhall which might escape notice at a quick glance. The under-surface is covered with a bitumastic sealing compound, to protect it against corrosion as well as contributing something towards sound-deadening. A single key serves for all locks—ignition, doors and tailgate. Protecting the screen wipers against failure (when overloaded, for instance, by a heavy build-up of snow) is an automatic switch to put the motor out of circuit until the cause is removed.

In addition to four fuses protecting other services there is also a thermal interrupter in the lighting switch, which rapidly makes and breaks a faulty circuit. In the case of a head lamp fault, the beams would not be completely extinguished. This device also protects the horn circuit. Each front seat is adjustable for height and angle, although this involves some work with a spanner and repositioning distance pieces.

Included in a helpful and comprehensive owner's handbook is a lubrication diagram which must be a joy to the

Left: This tidy and simple engine compartment is easily reached beneath a wide bonnet with hinged prop. A sensibly large screenwash reservoir is provided, and the scuttle vent flap for admitting fresh air to the interior has alternative degrees of opening. Right: With the rear seat raised, plenty of space remains for luggage. The spare wheel stows neatly in a well behind the right wheel arch

do-it-yourself home mechanic. Apart from periodic checks of the sump dipstick, little is required of him. Engine oil changes are suggested at 3,000-mile intervals, checks of oil level in other components and an oil filter element change every 6,000, but there are only four nipples on the suspension arm ball joints for attention every 12,000 miles or 12 months.

Without doubt, Vauxhall have made a long stride forward with this latest Victor. As an estate car it provides an abundance of practical carrying space which is easily reached through any of three doors. Yet in styling it is as handsome as any, without a suggestion of commercial austerity. As a family car it would suit many people better than an ordinary saloon, particularly when there are dogs to be carried. Easy to drive, mechanically refined and comfortably sprung, the Victor has a big future.

VAUXHALL VICTOR ESTATE CAR

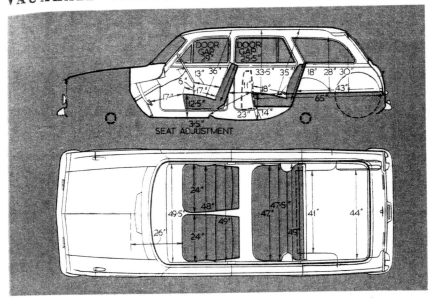

Scale ⅛in. to 1ft. Driving seat in central position. Cushions uncompressed.

PERFORMANCE

(Figures in brackets were recorded with 6 cwt load on board).

ACCELERATION TIMES (mean):
Speed range, Gear Ratios and Time in Sec.

M.p.h.	4·13 to 1	5·59 to 1	8·79 to 1	13·57 to 1
10—30			8·6	5·8 (6·6)	—
20—40	11·2	8·6 (10·9)	6·8	—
30—50	13·0 (16·1)	10·7 (13·5)	—	—
40—60	16·3 (22·6)	14·5 (18·9)	—	—
50—70	25·7	—	—	—

From rest through gears to:
- 30 m.p.h. .. 6·0 (7·2) sec.
- 40 „ .. 9·7 (12·0) „
- 50 „ .. 14·9 (19·2) „
- 60 „ .. 23·7 (31·3) „
- 70 „ .. 40·6 „

Standing quarter mile 21·8 sec. (24·1).

MAXIMUM SPEEDS ON GEARS:

Gear		m.p.h.	k.p.h.
Top	(mean)	77·2	124·3
	(best)	78·0	125·6
3rd	..	65	105
2nd	..	40	65
1st	..	26	42

TRACTIVE EFFORT (by Tapley meter):

	Pull (lb per ton)	Equivalent gradient
Top	195	1 in 11·4
Third	270	1 in 8·2
Second	420	1 in 5·2

BRAKES (at 30 m.p.h. in neutral):

Pedal load in lb	Retardation	Equiv. stopping distance in ft.
25	0·19g (0·12g)	159 (250)
50	0·38g (0·31g)	80 (97)
75	0·53g (0·40g)	57 (75)
100	0·76g (0·53g)	40 (57)
110	0·84g (0·61g)	35·9 (50)
120	— (0·68g)*	— (44)

*(Not maximum possible)

SPEEDOMETER CORRECTION m.p.h.:

Car speedometer	10	20	30	40	50	60	70	80
True speed	10	19	28	37	47	57	66	76

FUEL CONSUMPTION (at steady speeds in top gear):

30 m.p.h.	..	44·9 m.p.g.
40 „	..	41·2 „
50 „	..	36·4 „
60 „	..	31·2 „
70 „	..	26·3 „

Overall fuel consumption for 1,095 miles, 25·9 m.p.g. (10·9 litres per 100 km.).

Approximate normal range: 24–33 m.p.g. (11·8–8·6 litres per 100 km.).

Fuel: Premium grades.

TEST CONDITIONS: Weather: Dry and still.
Air temperature, 45 deg. F.
Model described in *The Autocar* of 15 September 1961.

STEERING: Turning circle:
Between kerbs: L, 33ft 11in.; R, 35ft 1in.
Between walls: L, 36ft 1in.; R, 37ft 3in.
Turns of steering wheel from lock to lock, 3·5.

DATA

PRICE (basic), with four-door estate car body, £590.
British purchase tax, £271 13s 1d.
Total (in Great Britain), £861 13s 1d.
Extras:
Four-speed gearbox £17 10s. Separate front seats £14 11s 8d. Heater £15 15s. Radio £20 15s 8d. Aerial £1 19s 6d. Screenwash £2 19s 6d. Wing mirrors (each) £1 5s. Anti-mist panel £1 15s. Fog and spot lamps (each) £3 17s 6d. Safety belts (each, front) £4 19s 6d. Glove box lock 8s 6d.
(Prices include purchase tax where applicable.)

ENGINE: Capacity, 1,508 c.c. (92 cu. in.).
Number of cylinders, 4 in line.
Bore and stroke, 79·37 × 76·20 mm (3·125 × 3·0in.).
Valve gear, overhead, pushrods and rockers.
Compression ratio, 8·1 to 1.
B.h.p. 49·5 (net) at 4,600 r.p.m. (B.h.p. per ton laden 42·9).
Torque, 85·6 lb ft at 2,200 r.p.m.
M.p.h. per 1,000 r.p.m. in top gear, 16·9.

WEIGHT: (With 5 gal fuel), 20·1 cwt (2,254 lb).
Weight distribution (per cent): F, 51·3; R, 48·7.
Laden as tested, 23·1 cwt (2,590 lb).
Lb per c.c. (laden), 1·7.

BRAKES: Type, Lockheed hydraulic.
Drum dimensions: F and R, 8in. diameter; 1·5in. wide.
Total swept area, 151 sq. in. (131 sq. in. per ton laden).

TYRES: 5·90–13in. Michelin tubeless.
Pressures (p.s.i.): F, 24; R, 24 (normal conditions) F, 24; R, 30 (fully laden).

TANK CAPACITY: 10 Imperial gallons.
Oil sump, 7·5 pints.
Cooling system, 11·75 pints (plus 1·5 pints if heater fitted).

DIMENSIONS: Wheelbase, 8ft 4in.
Track: F, 4ft 2·75in.; R, 4ft 3·12in.
Length (overall), 14ft 5·25in.
Width, 5ft 4in.
Height, 4ft 10in.
Ground clearance, 6·5in.
Frontal area, 19 sq. ft. (approximately).

ELECTRICAL SYSTEM: 12-volt; 38 ampère-hour battery.
Headlamps, 50–40 watt bulbs.

SUSPENSION: Front, coil springs and wishbones, telescopic dampers, anti-roll bar.
Rear, live-axle, half-elliptic leaf springs, telescopic dampers.

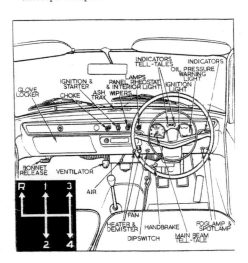

25

VAUXHALL
+
WEBER
+
BRABHAM
=
WORTHWHILE PERFORMANCE INCREASE

Deciding that we really ought to practise what we preach we looked around for ways of tweaking the office hack (a 1964 Vauxhall Victor Estate). Apart from anything else, lately we have been bolting on so many extra bits for test we felt it could do with some additional power to pull the extra weight about. The poor old thing is used quite a lot for towing racing cars, vintage cars, and boats, so we couldn't afford to sacrifice any of its power low down and, as the Estate is hardly a racer anyway, we decided to settle for something fairly mild which would improve the middle range power for overtaking and affect the fuel consumption as little as possible.

An obvious choice seemed to be a Brabham Weber conversion with possibly at a later date a polished cylinder head. For only £29 10s. 0d. and a £5 5s. 0d. fitting charge, Brabham will set you up with a special cast aluminium manifold, and 28/36 DCD carb, plus 35/- for an air cleaner, which is to be recommended if only to stop things "dropping in the works".

The Victor was duly presented at the Brabham establishment in Woking, Surrey early one morning and Ron Loneragan, taken off preparing a new Viva GT, was given the job of giving our car a little more steam.

First, the existing inlet manifold and exhaust system was removed and the hole in the exhaust manifold which had formed the hot-spot had to be filled. This was done by brazing in the head of an old valve, quite a tricky job in cast iron. Next, the throttle linkage was removed from the old carb and, apart from opening out the hole a little, the operating arm was fitted straight on to the Weber.

The exhaust manifold had by now cooled, and it was replaced on the car followed by the new manifold and carb. It was now a question of connecting up the fuel lines, choke and throttle linkage. This, though, was not quite as simple as it sounds. The fuel line had to be cut short, and a short piece of nylon piping used to connect up to the carb, as the union points downwards, rather than straight forward as on the standard unit. The linkage needed quite a lot of adjustment to ensure that the second butterfly would open fully, as we now needed more movement than previously and it was operating over a more acute angle. The choke was now all that remained; a slight snag cropped up here as on the Victor it pulls from the right and the Weber has to be pulled from the left. Ron got round this by fitting a new, longer, inner cable and bending-up a piece of piping in a loop to extend the outer and reverse the direction of pull.

Now we came to the tricky part, and the reason why Brabham insist that all their conversions should be carried out on their premises. There are a total of eight, yes eight, different jets in a DCD Weber and each one must be correct for that particular engine. They start off knowing pretty well what it will want, but it is impossible to get it absolutely correct without tuning it on your car. The beauty of a Weber, though, is that once it is really right it will stay that way almost for ever. But it MUST start off right.

After some changing-over of the main and slow running jets, Ron seemed reasonably pleased and armed with an exhaust gas analyser we set off for a test run. Having just got it really warm we opened it up on quite a short straight and quickly reached an indicated 70 in third and well over 90 in top. This was considerably better than it had ever done before, and we decided to call it a day. All that remained now was to try it against the stop watch but that could wait for a later date. In all the job had taken about three-quarters of a day. If you have a Victor and would like to have the edge on that one in front of you, then we suggest that it would be £36 10s. 0d. well spent.

Merely driving the Victor home was enough to make us realise that it was a lot quicker after Mr. Brabham's merry men had finished with it than before. The speedometer needle shot off the clock after about the same period of time as it had previously needed to reach about eighty, and what used to be, to all intents and purposes, the maximum speed attainable on any but long straights could now be considered a cruising speed.

With no attention or modification to the valve gear the speeds in the intermediate ratios hardly altered, but quite clearly a good deal was knocked off the acceleration times. But the most startling improvement was to the car's top-gear performance: the step-off from, say, fifty in top gear suddenly became as brisk as it had previously been in third. For a real appreciation of how much better the thing goes, have a look at the performance figures: a mean acceleration from rest to sixty of only fractionally over fifteen seconds makes it unusually quick by estate car standards, and it is a hard car to catch for most saloons under two litres. In modified form the car gets to 70 m.p.h. in three seconds less than the standard model needs to reach sixty, while in terms of top speed very nearly ten miles an hour has been tacked on. Cruising speed? So far as the power is concerned, anything up to just over eighty can be held almost indefinitely, but regrettably a prop-shaft vibration sets in at a bit below this speed which makes fast motoring of this sort a bit of a bind. For this reason, and the fact that we have yet to find a really satisfactory way of stopping the car from high speeds—it is the standard drum-braked version, to which we have added a servo and are also experimenting with various linings—we tend to bowl along at about seventy or a bit over. This is pleasant enough, covers the ground at an acceptable rate and yet does not present too many disadvantages in terms of noise or thirst.

So far as thirst is concerned, it is interesting that the modifications, and the increased use of even more performance, haven't made a particularly frightening difference to the fuel consumption. As standard we used to get a regular 24·2 m.p.g.: nowadays we have found that the figures have been swapped round—we now get a steady 22.4! A good big fuel tank means that the car has a really useful range on this basis, while you can cruise at something in the low seventies and still be able to listen to the radio in comfort.

In terms of roadholding we have found that the Victor is well suited to extra performance. The car adopts a pretty fair angle of heel when cornered fast but all four wheels stick down well, and with a bit of practice you can fling it about in fine style.

A peek at the performance figures will make it clear that, not surprisingly the Weber makes most difference to the top end of the performance range, chopping seven seconds off the 0—60 time and an incredible seventeen seconds or so off the 0—70 figure!

We can really recommend this as a conversion—the Victor has covered a few thousand miles since Brabham's men did the job and we have experienced no untoward difficulties—in fact, no trouble at all as far as the engine or the conversion is concerned. The important address is Jack Brabham Conversions Ltd., 131-139 Goldsworth Road, Woking, Surrey.

Cars on Test

VAUXHALL VICTOR ESTATE (BRABHAM CONVERTED)

PERFORMANCE

Figures in brackets relate to standard car.

Maximum speed 92 m.p.h. (83.6)

ACCELERATION
0—30	4.4	(6.5)
0—40	7.0	(10.1)
0—50	9.8	(14.5)
0—60	15.1	(22.2)
0—70	19.5	(36.2)

Fuel consumption 22.4 (24.2) driven hard.

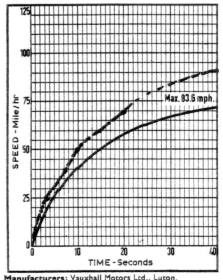

Manufacturers: Vauxhall Motors Ltd., Luton, Bedfordshire.
Conversion by: Jack Brabham Conversions Ltd., 131-139 Goldsworth Road, Woking, Surrey.

Vauxhall Victor Estate Car (de luxe)

CLEAN and attractive lines always put testers in a good mood. The Vauxhall Victor Estate Car is more than merely good-looking, however. It is a thoroughly satisfactory dual-purpose vehicle (although people who habitually carry awkward or dirty loads might prefer the less de luxe version) or a comfortable family saloon with lots of baggage space. Acceleration is little affected by the lower gearing and extra weight, and the mean maximum speed was actually 4 m.p.h. up on the saloon. Except for some body roll on corners, the car handles well and the steering is light and positive; even when lightly loaded, wheel adhesion is excellent. More petrol is needed for the Estate Car's pleasantly brisk performance than for the saloon; both constant speed and overall consumption figures show it to be a little greedier. The car sets as high a standard in nearly every aspect of its behaviour as its good looks suggest, and a splendid gearchange will attract people who enjoy driving.

Four smooth cylinders

WITHIN the same wheelbase and overall length, the Victor Estate Car weighs 1½ cwt. more than the saloon. From the door pillars forwards, it is identical, with the same 1,508 c.c. four-cylinder engine which idled so evenly that in traffic halts it was sometimes thought to have stalled. It transmitted its 49½ b.h.p. evenly through the optional four-speed gearbox which costs £14 10s. 0d. more than the standard three-speed. The four-speed box, together with its exemplary central change and synchromesh throughout, is well worth the extra outlay.

The crisp, clean lines of the Victor Estate Car. Reversing lights, fog and spot, and left-hand wing mirror are extras. The chrome strip along the body sides identifies the de luxe model.

In Brief

Price (including 4-speed gearbox as tested) £677 plus purchase tax £141 12s. 1d. equals £818 12s. 1d.	
Capacity	1,508 c.c.
Unladen kerb weight	20¼ cwt.
Acceleration:	
20-40 m.p.h. in top gear	11.4 sec.
0-50 m.p.h. through gears	14.4 sec.
Maximum top gear gradient	1 in 12.8
Maximum speed	80.0 m.p.h.
Overall fuel consumption	24.0 m.p.g.
Touring fuel consumption	30.5 m.p.g.
Gearing: 16.65 m.p.h. in top gear at 1,000 r.p.m.	

The Motor Road Tests

MAKE: Vauxhall   **TYPE:** Victor Estate Car de Luxe
MAKERS: Vauxhall Motors Ltd. Luton, Beds.

ROAD TEST • No. 11/63

TEST DATA:

World copyright reserved; no unauthorized reproduction in whole or in part.

CONDITIONS: Weather: dry, mild with a light wind (Temperature 46°-48°F., Barometer 29·5 in. Hg.) Surface: Damp concrete and tarmacadam. Fuel: Premium grade pump petrol (98 Octane by Research Method)

MAXIMUM SPEEDS
Flying Quarter Mile
Mean lap speed around banked circuit 80·0 m.p.h.
Best one-way ¼-mile time equals .. 83·2 m.p.h.

"Maximile" Speed: (Timed quarter mile after one mile accelerating from rest).
Mean of four opposite runs .. 79·9 m.p.h.
Best one-way time equals . .. 80·2 m.p.h.

Speed in Gears
Max. speed in 3rd gear .. .. 63 m.p.h.
Max. speed in 2nd gear .. .. 42 m.p.h.
Max. speed in 1st gear .. .. 27 m.p.h.

ACCELERATION TIMES From standstill
0-30 m.p.h. .. .. 5·9 sec.
0-40 m.p.h. .. .. 9·5 sec.
0-50 m.p.h. .. .. 14·4 sec.
0-60 m.p.h. .. .. 25·9 sec.
0-70 m.p.h. .. .. 39·7 sec.
Standing quarter mile .. .. 22·4 sec.

ACCELERATION TIMES on upper ratios
	Top gear	3rd gear
10-30 m.p.h.	10·1 sec.	6·6 sec.
20-40 m.p.h.	11·4 sec.	7·2 sec.
30-50 m.p.h.	14·4 sec.	9·7 sec.
40-60 m.p.h.	17·7 sec.	14·6 sec.
50-70 m.p.h.	21·8 sec.	

HILL CLIMBING
Max. gradient climbable at steady speed.
Top gear .. 1 in 12·8 (Tapley 175 lb./ton)
Third gear.. 1 in 8·5 (Tapley 260 lb./ton)
Second gear 1 in 5·6 (Tapley 400 lb./ton)

FUEL CONSUMPTION
Overall Fuel Consumption for 1,752 miles, 73 gallons, equals 24·0 m.p.g. (11·75 litres/100 km.).

Touring Fuel Consumption (m.p.g. at steady speed midway between 30 m.p.h. and maximum, less 5% allowance for acceleration) 30·5 m.p.g.
Fuel tank capacity (maker's figure) 10 gallons

Direct top gear
42¼ m.p.g. .. at constant 30 m.p.h. on level
38¼ m.p.g. .. at constant 40 m.p.h. on level
33½ m.p.g. .. at constant 50 m.p.h. on level
30½ m.p.g. .. at constant 60 m.p.h. on level
25¼ m.p.g. .. at constant 70 m.p.h. on level
21 m.p.g. .. at maximum speed of approximately 30 m.p.h.

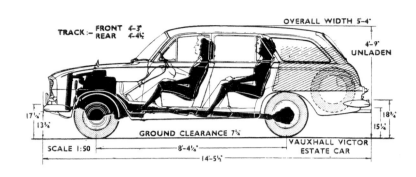

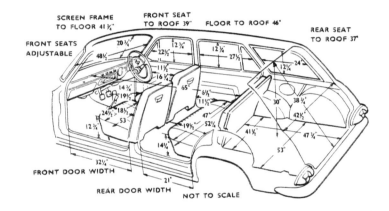

BRAKES
Deceleration and equivalent stopping distance from 30 m.p.h.
1·0 g with 90 lb. pedal pressure.. .. 30 ft.
0·94 g with 75 lb. pedal pressure.. .. 32 ft.
0·58 g with 50 lb. pedal pressure.. .. 51·5 ft.
0·34 g with 25 lb. pedal pressure.. .. 88 ft.

STEERING
Turning circle between kerbs:
Left .. .. 31¾ ft.
Right .. .. 30¼ ft.
Turns of steering wheel from lock to lock 3¼

INSTRUMENTS
Speedometer at 30 m.p.h. .. .. 2% fast
Speedometer at 60 m.p.h. .. .. 4% fast
Distance recorder .. .. accurate

WEIGHT
Kerb weight (unladen, but with oil, coolant and fuel for approximately 50 miles) .. 20¼ cwt.
Front/rear distribution of kerb weight 51/49
Weight laden as tested .. .. .. 24 cwt.

Specification

Engine
Cylinders 4
Bore .. .. 79·37 mm.
Stroke .. .. 76·2 mm.
Cubic capacity .. .. .. 1,508 c.c.
Piston area .. .. .. 30·7 sq. in.
Valves .. .. .. Pushrod O.H.V.
Compression ratio .. 8·1/1 (7·0/1 optional)
Carburetter .. .. .. Zenith 34VN
Fuel pump .. .. AC-Delco mechanical
Ignition timing control .. Vacuum and centrifugal
Oil filter .. .. .. AC-Delco by-pass
Maximum power (net) .. 49·5 b.h.p.
at .. .. .. 4,600 r.p.m.
Maximum torque (gross) .. 85·6 lb. ft.
at .. .. .. 2,200 r.p.m.
Piston speed at maximum b.h.p. 2,300 ft./min.

Transmission
Clutch .. Borg and Beck, 7·25 AC single dry plate
Top gear (s/m) .. .. .. 4·125
3rd gear (s/m) .. .. .. 5·589
2nd gear (s/m) .. .. .. 8·786
1st gear (s/m) .. .. .. 13·571
Reverse.. .. .. .. 12·581
Propeller shaft .. .. Single piece, open
Final drive .. .. Hypoid bevel
Top gear m.p.h. at 1,000 r.p.m. 16·65
Top gear m.p.h. at 1,000 ft./min. piston speed 33·4

Chassis
Brakes Lockheed hydraulic (2 L.S. at front)
Brake dimensions 8 in. dia. x 1 7/16 in. wide
Friction areas 92 sq. in. of lining working on 150·6 sq. in. rubbed area of drums
Suspension
  Front Independent, by coil springs, transverse wishbones and anti-roll torsion bar
  Rear Rigid axle and semi-elliptic leaf springs
Shock absorbers : Telescopic
Steering gear : Burman recirculating ball
Tyres : 5·90—13 6-ply tubeless

Right: The de luxe Estate Car has leather upholstery with a silvery finish. The seats are more comfortable than their shape suggests but the roll on top of the facia caused reflections in the screen. The bonnet catch is below the facia on the left. *Below:* The pedals are well positioned but the heater controls under the facia are far away and fumbly. The handbrake releases with a twist.

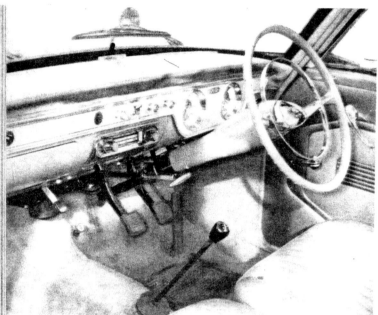

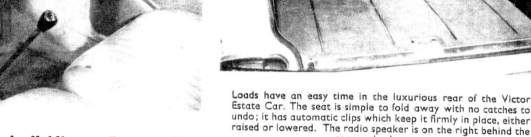

Loads have an easy time in the luxurious rear of the Victor Estate Car. The seat is simple to fold away with no catches to undo; it has automatic clips which keep it firmly in place, either raised or lowered. The radio speaker is on the right behind the spare wheel cover.

Vauxhall Victor Estate Car

There is some whine on the indirects but the ratios are well chosen and the car reaches really useful speeds on them. With a maximum of 27 m.p.h., first is handy for quick getaway but a start on a 1 in 3 hill was impossible; it was willing enough on a 1 in 4 gradient. The synchromesh is almost unbeatable but the lever has to be moved quite a long way between changes; first and second positions, which have to be engaged against a spring, are rather far from the driver.

Acceleration is not much affected by a back axle ratio of 4.125:1 instead of the saloon's 3.9. With 5.90x13 6-ply tyres the Estate Car does 16.65 m.p.h. per 1,000 r.p.m. in top gear, against the saloon's 17.3 so that it achieves a mean maximum speed of 80 m.p.h. at 4,800 r.p.m. and the saloon reaches its 76.2 at 4,400 r.p.m. It is only at or near top speed that engine noise rises above a low hum and it never sounds fussy or hurried. Wind noise is not great either, and it was possible to cruise the Victor for long distances at an indicated 80 m.p.h. quite tirelessly. At this speed it was only necessary to turn the radio up a shade but the car's overall quietness was spoilt by an exhaust resonance, particularly on the overrun. It was audible outside as a crisp note, but inside it was an annoying buzz. The body was free from road noise except on coarse tarmacadam which set up a high-pitched vibration. On very rough surfaces a few rattles suggested slight lack of stiffness round the tailgate.

The recirculatory ball steering is light and has a pleasant self-centring action. There is some sponginess—particularly approaching full lock—but on the whole it is satisfactory. The brakes are light and progressive but could be made to fade under severe conditions. The handbrake worked effectively on a 1 in 3 test hill. It has to be reached for under the facia, which was difficult for drivers who sat well back and wore seat belts.

Body roll

WITH its weight distribution nearer 50/50 than the saloon, the Victor Estate Car's understeer is perhaps not so marked. Body roll on corners, however, remains a feature of the handling although, to cope with loads, the suspension is slightly stiffer. Lightly laden, there is some rear-axle hop but even on very bumpy corners this does not upset the car's stability as much as might be expected. With such a large area exposed to sidewinds, the car is sometimes thrown slightly off course in strong gusts. There are no objectionable characteristics in the road behaviour, and even when cornered at its limit, no vices develop suddenly. The ride is quite soft and well-insulated, but damping is good and there is no wavy motion which might upset sensitive passengers and little nose-dive on braking as on some softly sprung cars.

Inside, the Vauxhall is perhaps less tasteful than outside, the silvery finish on the upholstery seeming out of place in a car with such solid virtues. The individual front seats are comfortable and provided enough adjustment for all sizes of driver. The cushions are quite firm and the angle of the squab suggests that a good deal of thought has gone into the design. The armrest in the door is rather small but the comfort of the driving position emphasized the Victor's suitability for extended periods of occupation.

Useful features

THE facia is finished somewhat gaudily with bright metal strips and the light coloured material of the padded roll along the top reflected badly on the windscreen at night and even threw a grey ghost on the bottom half in daylight. The instruments can be seen easily enough although they are casually calibrated and set vertically in the panel. The glove locker's let-down lid opens flat which is a useful feature but it is the sole receptacle provided for the front occupants. The optional parcels shelf would be worth a buyer's consideration. Switchgear is not very conveniently placed in the middle of the facia and the movement as well as the location of some of the switches has to be memorized. The windscreen wiper switch, for example, has to be pulled for washing and turned for wiping. While it is useful to have both actions incorporated in the one switch, it can be confusing to a driver not used to the car. The flasher switch is on the right of the steering column and works with a sturdy sounding click. Forward visibility over the flat bonnet is good and the screen wipers clear a wide area.

On the de luxe model tested, the floor is neatly carpeted front and rear and the space at the back has metal strips to make loading easy. The comfortable back seat conceals the jack clipped neatly to the floor and rear passengers sit slightly higher than those at the front. Three people can occupy the back seat and when it is folded down there is a flat deck measuring 68 in. to the tailgate. This does not mean, however, that the back will hold a large box 68 in. long because the slope of the tailgate diminishes the available length quite a lot near the roof. Additional de luxe equipment includes a cover for the spare wheel, which takes up surprisingly little space tucked aft of the right rear wheel arch, and a carpet-lined pocket in the opposite rear quarter. The tailgate is hinged to open upwards automatically but on the car tested the springs did not raise it high enough, and although light to lift, a person of medium height straightening up from loading the interior could knock his head on it.

Effective heater

THE Victor was an easy starter from cold and warming up was rapid. The heater controls take a little learning and the booster fan has inherited a loud noise which Vauxhall seem curiously reluctant to banish. Although not so bad as it once was, it has been an integral part of every Victor heater for much too long. Adjustment of the heater is a critical matter, a little movement of the difficult-to-get-at levers make a great difference in the amount of heat delivered. Both in heating and demisting however, the installation is powerful and effective, although rear seat passengers get no more than their share of warmth.

Maintenance has been reduced to four points which need attention every 30,000 miles or every 30 months, which enhances the car's value for people to whom time spent in the garage means time lost. Although the overall fuel consumption of 24 m.p.g. may not at first appeal to the commercially minded, the less enthusiastic driver would probably record a figure nearer that of our Touring Fuel Consumption of 30½ m.p.g.

Vauxhall have a highly competitive car in the Victor Estate. At a price (without extras) of just over £800 including tax (the more austere version is £66 cheaper at £738) it represents outstanding value for money and the only extra which most people would consider almost essential is the four-speed gearbox. The heater is standard. Pleasant to drive as well as practical to use, the Victor is popular in its three saloon guises and its success as an Estate Car seems assured.

Oil, water, battery, and hydraulic reservoirs are easy to get at under the wide-opening bonnet which it is necessary to prop open. The vacuum-operated screenwasher unit is on the right.

Coachwork and Equipment

Starting handle	None
Battery mounting	Under bonnet
Jack	Screwed pedestal type
Jacking Points	2 each side underneath body
Standard tool kit: Jack, jack handle, and wheel nut spanner.	
Exterior lights: 2 headlamps, 2 sidelamps, 2 stop/tail lamps, 1 number plate light.	
Number of electrical fuses: 4 fuses (also thermal circuit breaker in lighting switch).	
Direction indicators	Self-cancelling flashers
Windscreen wipers	Electrical, self-parking
Windscreen washers: Vacuum operated (standard equipment on de luxe).	
Sun visors	Two
Instruments: Speedometer with decimal, total distance recorder, water temperature gauge, fuel gauge.	
Warning lights: Oil pressure, ignition, main beam, turn indicators.	
Locks:	
With ignition key: Ignition/starter switch, front doors, tail door	
With other keys	None
Glove lockers	One in facia with lid
Map pockets	None
Parcel shelves	One optional
Ashtrays: One on top of facia, one behind each front seat	
Cigar lighters	Optional
Interior lights: One in roof with courtesy switches in front doors and tail door	
Interior heater	Standard
Car radio	Optional
Extras available: Four-speed gearbox, radio, fog lamps, roof rack, safety belts, anti-mist panels, reversing lights, cigar lighter.	
Upholstery material	Leather
Floor covering	Carpet
Exterior colours standardized: 15, 9 single, and 6 two-tone	
Alternative body styles: Victor Saloon variants and Victor Estate car	

Maintenance

Sump	7½ pints, S.A.E. 20 or 20w.
Gearbox	2.1 pints, S.A.E. 90
Rear axle	2¼ pints, S.A.E. 90 hypoid
Steering gear lubricant	S.A.E. 90
Cooling system capacity: 13¼ pints (2 drain taps)	
Chassis lubrication: By grease gun every 30,000 miles to 4 points	
Ignition timing	9° b.t.d.c.
Contact breaker gap	0.019 in.-0.021 in.
Sparking plug type	AC 44/5V
Sparking plug gap	0.028 in.-0.032 in.
Valve timing: Inlet opens 19.6° b.t.d.c. and closes 60.6° a.b.d.c.; exhaust opens 51.6° b.b.d.c. and closes 28.6° a.t.d.c.	
Tappet clearances (hot): Inlet and exhaust	0.013 in.
Front wheel toe-in	1/16 to 3/32 in.
Camber angle	¼° to 1¼°
Castor angle	½° to 3¼°
Steering swivel pin inclination	5° to 6°
Tyre pressures: Front and rear	24 lb. Up to 30 lb. when fully loaded
Brake fluid: Lockheed Super Heavy Duty to S.A.E. spec. R3	
Battery type and capacity	12-volt, 38 amp.-hr.

Vauxhall Victor 101 estate car 1,595 c.c.

ONE of the most successful estate cars to gain favour in its own right was undoubtedly the Vauxhall Victor of what must now be termed pre-101 vintage. Its well-balanced lines swayed many families away from the ordinary saloon styling, even when they had no real need for its dual-purpose capacity. When the model was rebodied for last year's London motor show it took on much more than just a new mantle over the old limbs, for a large number of detail engineering changes were introduced. These have helped it to assume a new, more refined character as well.

The new styling, and of course the mechanical changes, are common to the whole Victor range from standard to de luxe models (with the super in between). Estate cars can be ordered only to super or de luxe specifications, the difference being that the latter costs £85 more but includes the optional separate front seats, heater and screenwasher which otherwise would add £30 to the invoice. In addition, de luxe cars have better quality trim; and our test car also had two other mechanical options and a number of accessories which altogether brought its value up to just over £931.

Basically the Victor has a three-speed gearbox with a steering column change and 9in. dia. drum brakes all round. However, for about £15 extra a four-speed all-synchromesh box with a central floor change is available; and for almost the same price disc front brakes with a vacuum-servo are another option. For an estate car which is going to be worked hard, both these items are desirable, because the extra intermediate ratio (first gears are much the same in both boxes) definitely helps the car to get along, especially with a load, and the braking system as tested always gives superb and reassuring stopping power with no fade and very light pedal pressures.

PRICES	£
Estate car de luxe	725
Purchase tax	153
TOTAL (in G.B.)	878

How the Vauxhall Victor 101 estate car compares:

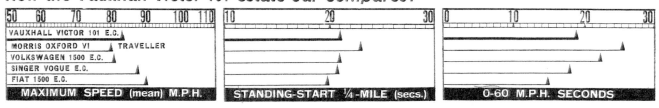

Only de luxe models have the separate front seats as standard. Note the curved doors which add 4in. to the rear shoulder room

Vauxhall Victor 101 estate car . . .

The power unit is a conventional in-line four with a modest 60 b.h.p. from nearly 1,600 c.c. It is a relatively slow revving engine, with its peak power at 4,600 r.p.m. and maximum torque at just over half this speed—2,400 r.p.m. Pulling power from low speeds is therefore very good, even with 5cwt of ballast in the back, and if one feels in a lazy mood there are no protests when trickling along in top, right down to 15 m.p.h. For performance, however, the gearbox must be used freely. It has a positive light change with powerful synchromesh that could never be beaten. The lever is slightly springy and its curious shape lets it clear the seats in their most forward position and still brings it within easy reach.

Ratios are well matched to the engine characteristics, with third being particularly useful. It has a maximum of about 60 m.p.h. which seems just right for getting past heavy commercial vehicles on the open road, and at the same time makes it a good gear for pressing on through twisting lanes in the country. First gear (and the clutch) made easy work of a restart on a 1-in-4 test hill. We also took off from 1-in-3, but this involved a good deal of clutch slipping to keep the revs up.

In traffic, the Victor is usually one of the quickest cars away. First can be slipped straight in while the wheels are still rolling, or extremely briskly when the lights have started to change. On slopes the pull-and-twist handle for the parking brake has plenty of bite for little effort and is released with a rapid fly-off action by a quick finger flick. It held facing either way on 1-in-3 and recorded a creditable 0·4g when tested for emergency stopping from 30 m.p.h.

On the road, one feels that the brakes would stop the car on a sixpence if required, and when too much thrust is put on the pedal the Victor practically stands up on its front bumper. Our measurements confirmed that 1·0g stopping was possible for the very reasonable load of 100lb; but with two up and no load the rear wheels locked at only 50lb, causing the tail to slew sharply to the right. With ballast on board as well this tendency would have been reduced or eliminated, but as the rear seatback jumped out of its clips at retardations above about 0·5g the load would also have shifted forward violently. These clips for holding the seat up are little plastic buttons which snap into metal plates, and a more positive locking system would be safer.

When tested for fade from 70 m.p.h., pedal pressure only increased from 40 to 45lb during 10 stops at 0·5g at approximately ¼-mile intervals. On strange roads the excellent stopping power helps one get along much more quickly with confidence.

Left: The tail-gate lifts clear of the body leaving the full width open for loading. Right: All engine accessories can be reached easily but the bonnet lid must be propped up with a stay

Make · VAUXHALL   Type · Victor 101 Estate Car (1,595 c.c.)
(Front engine, rear-wheel drive)

Manufacturer: Vauxhall Motors Ltd., Luton, Bedfordshire

Test Conditions
Weather ... Sunny intervals and snow showers with 0-2 m.p.h. wind
Temperature .... 1 deg. C. (34 deg. F.)
Barometer .... 30·10in. Hg.
Mainly dry tarmac and concrete surfaces

Weight
Kerb weight (with oil, water and half-full fuel tank) 21·4 cwt (2,395lb–1,088kg)
Font-rear distribution, per cent F. 49; R. 51
Laden as tested .... 24·4cwt (2,731lb–1,240kg)

Turning Circles
Between kerbs .... L. 33ft. 8in.; R. 33ft. 5in.
Between walls .... L. 36ft. 0in.; R. 35ft. 9in.
Turns of steering wheel lock to lock .... 4·5

FUEL CONSUMPTION

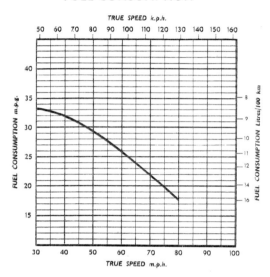

At Steady Speeds in Top:

30 m.p.h.	33·3	m.p.g.
40 "	32·0	"
50 "	29·4	"
60 "	25·9	"
70 "	22·0	"
80 "	17·9	"

Test Distance .... 1,540 miles
Overall Consumption .... 21·2 m.p.g.
(13·4 litres/100 km.)
Estimated (DIN) .... 23·6 m.p.g.
(12·0 litres/100 km.)
Normal range .... 20–25 m.p.g.
(14·1–11·3 litres/100 km.)
Grade .... Premium
(96–98 octane RM)
OIL CONSUMPTION (SAE 20)
12,000 m.p.g.

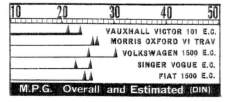

M.P.G. Overall and Estimated (DIN)
VAUXHALL VICTOR 101 E.C.
MORRIS OXFORD VI TRAV
VOLKSWAGEN 1500 E.C.
SINGER VOGUE E.C.
FIAT 1500 E.C.

MAXIMUM SPEEDS AND ACCELERATION TIMES

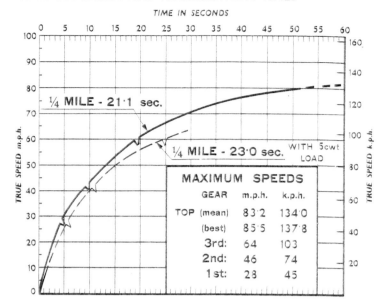

¼ MILE – 21·1 sec.
¼ MILE – 23·0 sec. WITH 5cwt LOAD

MAXIMUM SPEEDS

GEAR	m.p.h.	k.p.h.
TOP (mean)	83·2	134·0
(best)	85·5	137·8
3rd:	64	103
2nd:	46	74
1st:	28	45

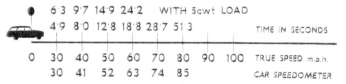

6·3 9·7 14·9 24·2 WITH 5cwt LOAD
4·9 8·0 12·8 18·8 28·7 51·3 TIME IN SECONDS

0 30 40 50 60 70 80 90 100 TRUE SPEED m.p.h.
   30 41 52 63 74 85   CAR SPEEDOMETER

Speed range, gear ratios and time in seconds

m.p.h.	Top (4·13)	Third (5·59)	Second (8·79)	First (13·55)
10—30	...	8·0	4·6	—
20—40	10·6	7·4	5·3	—
30—50	11·6	8·0	—	—
40—60	12·8	11·0	—	—
50—70	15·6	—	—	—
60—80	33·7	—	—	—

BRAKES (from 30 m.p.h. in neutral)

Pedal load	Retardation	Equiv. distance
25lb	0·40g	75ft
50lb	0·80g	38ft
75lb	0·90g	33·4ft
100lb	1·0g	30·1ft
Hand brake	0·40g	75ft

CLUTCH Pedal load and travel—42lb and 5in.

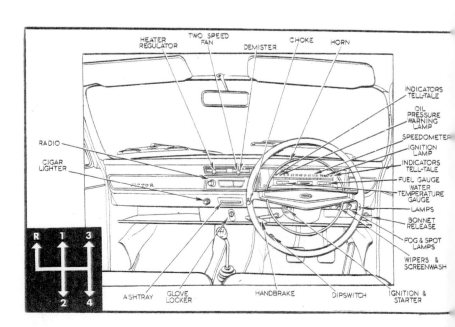

34

The lines of the 101 do not please everyone, but the new body does give much more room inside without any significant increase in overall dimensions

The suspension of the Victor 101 feels much stiffer than its predecessor's, for that car tended to float and pitch quite a lot. The new one is not harsh but taut, with well damped wheel movements, yet it still has the ability to ride sharp undulations evenly. On our *pavé* and some farm tracks we visited it was good for its type, with none of the bucking and directional disturbances that some cars display, but at the same time the live back axle could not be forgotten as it thumped under the floor. Structurally the car felt much more rigid than other Victors and there were no rattles.

On corners there is a lot of body roll, but the seats help one stay in place. At normal speeds the handling is neutral, the car taking the line one expects, but towards the limit in the wet the front drifts wide unless more lock is applied. On sharp turns taken fast and suddenly, a rear wheel lifts, causing the tail to skip round. Vauxhall draw on several manufacturers for their supply of tyres and our car was on the latest Goodyear G.8s. For conventional tyres we were considerably surprised at how good they were; it seemed almost impossible to spin the wheels in the wet even when we were measuring the acceleration in falling snow.

Steering is light in the Vauxhall tradition, but not quite as light as we remembered the last car's, possibly due to the slightly fatter section tyres fitted to estate cars. Parking in a tight gap is no chore and, although there are 4½ turns between locks, the small diameter wheel (it feels even smaller than it measures) is easy to manipulate. There is no lost motion and the whole mechanism feels much more positive than it has in the past.

Generally the noise level inside the car has been much reduced. There is thick bulkhead insulation to cut down engine noise and under the carpets is a composite layer of felt and foam rubber. Only towards maximum revs does the engine make itself obtrusive with that harshness which characterizes a three-main-bearing four-cylinder. There is an audible whine from the indirect gears, especially third on the over-run, but this is subdued. Wind noise is very low, and the new front quarterlights can be opened at speed without a deafening roar or whistle. It is quieter with them shut, but not annoying to use one for ventilation on motorways.

One of the good features of the Vauxhall heater has always been the efficient way it can produce warm air after only a few hundred yards from a cold start. This is still true of the new system with its simplified controls and ducts for the rear compartment, but we found that, if anything, too much air was bled to the back and the driver's left foot got cold. If we owned this model we would either stuff a duster up the right-hand duct or remove it altogether. In the back, however, there is a good flow of warm air round the feet to stop Granny complaining.

There is no provision for splitting the temperature control above and below the facia and on a long night run we wished we could have arranged a cool face breeze to keep us alert, without freezing from the waist down.

Looking round the interior one can see the strong American influence in the styling of the instruments and trim. The distinctively shaped switch knobs, with their clever double actions, are still there and the new speedometer is clear and easy to read. The cubby-hole now lies in the middle of the car just below the dashboard and has a sliding lid which can be locked. It forms a roomy cache for valuables like a camera, portable radio or touring documents. There is plenty of extra shelf space for maps, handbags and all the other oddments.

The new front seats are soft and comfortable, with good contours. Initially, there seemed to be too much pressure in the small of one's back, but after 1,500 miles it felt less and we would expect the upholstery to settle. For driving, the cushion holds one's thighs at the correct angle to attack the pedals, but passengers who like to slump more found theirs too short. In the back the seat is outstandingly good for an estate car, where often the padding is skimped to ease folding. The new 101 has an extra 4in. of shoulder room,

Porters' view of the rear compartment with the back seat folded. There is 5ft. 11in. of flat floor with a minimum width of 3ft. 4in. and room for a 4ft carry-cot right at the back even with the rear seats in use

35

making a real three-abreast bench, and there are shaped cutouts under the front seats which are carpet covered and fit one's shin and ankle line. There are no rear armrests, just an ashtray on each back door.

Folding the back seat is exceedingly simple; the cushion just lifts up and the back drops to engage in two tongues. There is then a flat, clear floor, carpeted and with aluminium runners, 5ft 11in. long—6in. more than on the previous model. The spare wheel sits in a well on the right with a neat zip-on cover. The back door is the full width of the body and lifts high on counter-sprung hinges to clear the opening completely and form a rain shield for loading. As it opens, it automatically switches on the interior lamp.

Like the tail-gate, the bonnet is the full width of the body, which makes it impossible to fit wing mirrors. To comply with the legal requirements, an outside mirror is mounted on the driver's door as standard, in addition to the interior one which, incidentally, can be turned over on its ball-joint to raise or lower it ¾in. Our car had a matching door mirror on the passenger side, but a large movement of the head was needed to look into it. Perhaps the step below the glass helped, but the back window did not get as grimy as on most estate cars.

Compared with the last Victor estate car we tested, which had larger wheels, this model is much lower geared at 16·9 m.p.h. per 1,000 r.p.m. instead of 18·1. Acceleration is therefore better and less affected by a load (0 to 70 m.p.h. now takes 28·7sec compared with 31·7), but the fuel consumption rate has increased substantially. The new body cannot be as windcheating as the old one, and our steady-speed consumption curve is about 15 per cent down. The overall figure of 21·2 m.p.g. represents a very varied test mileage of more than 1,500 including a weekend trip to South Wales when 24 m.p.g. was returned. Each time the tank was filled it blew back violently, so we deducted a gallon from our total to allow for these slops. With a tank capacity of 10gal, the effective range is therefore rather under 200 miles.

At night the headlamps are adequate for the performance of the car, but they were angled low to allow for the change in trim which a weight in the back would bring. No headlamp flasher is fitted.

The Vauxhall system of door locks continues, with the useful provision of an ignition switch which can be unlocked and used with the key removed, and doors which can be secured from outside without the key. The driver can therefore keep the car key on a ring with his others and not have them all jangling from the ignition, which is now tucked away on the steering column to simplify the fitting of an optional steering lock.

To drive about 300 miles virtually non-stop and still like a car is a good test. In the Victor we always felt secure, warm, comfortable and content. It has a natural motorway gait of just over 70 m.p.h. when one can listen to a play on the radio without straining, and on other trunk routes one can press along almost as well. The styling may excite controversy, but in its anatomy and performance it is a new and better car.

Specification: Vauxhall Victor 101 estate car

PERFORMANCE DATA
Top gear m.p.h. per 1,000 r.p.m. .... 16·9
Mean piston speed at max. power .... 2,300 ft/min.
Engine revs at mean max. speed .... 4,925 r.p.m.
B.h.p. per ton laden .... 49·4

▼ *Scale: 0·3in. to 1ft. Cushions uncompressed.*

ENGINE
Cylinders ... 4-in-line
Cooling system ... Water, pump, fan and thermostat
Bore ... 81·6mm (3·21in.)
Stroke ... 76·2mm (3·00in.)
Displacement ... 1,595 c.c. (97·4 cu. in.)
Valve gear ... Overhead, pushrods and rockers
Compression ratio ... 9-to-1; optional 7-to-1
Carburettor ... Zenith 34 IV downdraught
Fuel pump ... AC-Delco, mechanical
Oil filter ... AC-Delco, by-pass type
Max. power ... 60 b.h.p. (net) at 4,600 r.p.m.
Max. torque ... 86 lb. ft. (net) at 2,400 r.p.m.

TRANSMISSION
Clutch ... Borg and Beck, single dry plate, 8in. dia.
Gearbox ... Standard 3-speed all-synchromesh; optional extra 4-speed all-synchromesh
Gear ratios ... Top 1·0, Third 1·36, Second 2·13, (4-speed box) First 3·29, Reverse 3·04
Final drive ... Spiral Hypoid, 4·125 to 1

CHASSIS and BODY
Construction ... Integral with steel body

SUSPENSION
Front ... Independent, double wishbones, coil springs, telescopic dampers
Rear ... Live axle, half-elliptic leaf springs, telescopic dampers
Steering ... Recirculating-ball type
Turns, lock-to-lock 4·5
Wheel dia. ... 16·0in.

BRAKES
Type ... Girling drum standard; optional front discs and vacuum servo
Dimensions ... F 9·06in. dia. (discs), R 9·0in. dia. 1·75in. wide shoes
Swept area (discs) ... F 154 sq. in., R 99 sq. in. Total 253 sq. in. (208 sq. in. per ton laden)

WHEELS
Type ... Steel disc, 4 studs. 4in. wide rim
Tyres ... Goodyear G.8 tubeless; 5·90—13in. (various other makes may be supplied)

EQUIPMENT
Battery ... 12-volt 38-amp. hr.
Generator ... Lucas, 22 amp.
Headlamps ... Lucas sealed beam 60/45-watt
Reversing lamp ... Extra
Electric fuses ... 4 plus circuit breaker for lamps
Screen wipers ... Single-speed, self-parking
Screen washer ... Standard, vacuum-operated
Interior heater ... Standard, fresh-air
Safety belts ... Extra
Interior trim ... Ambla stretch plastic seats, p.v.c. headlining
Floor covering ... Woven pile carpet
Starting handle ... No provision
Jack ... Screw-pillar type
Jacking points ... 2 each side under sills
Other bodies ... Saloon

MAINTENANCE
Fuel tank ... 10·1 Imp. gallons (no reserve) (45·9 litres)
Cooling system ... 13·3 pints (including heater) (7·5 litres)
Engine sump ... 7·5 pints (4·3 litres) SAE 20 or 20W. Change oil every 3,000 miles. Change filter element every 6,000 miles.
Gearbox ... 2·4 pints SAE 80 No change necessary
Final drive ... 2·5 pints SAE 90 No change necessary
Grease ... 4 points every 30,000 miles
Tyre pressures ... F 24, R 24 p.s.i. (normal driving) F 24, R 30 p.s.i. (full load)

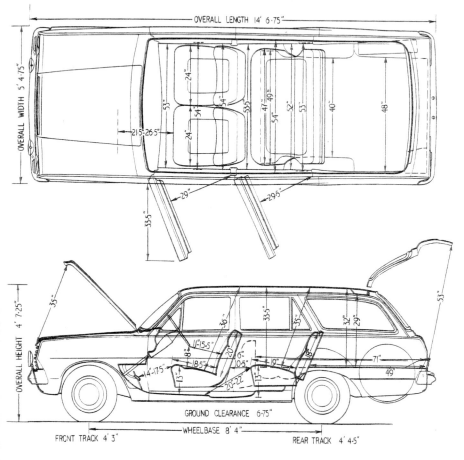

VAUXHALL VICTOR 101 AND VX4/90
INDEX TO REPAIR OPERATIONS

BODYWORK
BRAKES
CLUTCH
COOLING SYSTEM
ELECTRICAL SYSTEM
ENGINE
FRONT AXLE AND FRONT
   SUSPENSION

FUEL SUPPLY SYSTEM
GEARBOX
IGNITION
REAR AXLE AND REAR
   SUSPENSION
SHOCK ABSORBERS
STEERING
WHEELS AND TYRES

BODYWORK

Body is of integral construction, comprising deck, shell, bulkheads, front frame, rear longitudinals, front and rear cross-members etc. To assist body front-end repair, an assembly frame is available.

DOORS.—Detachable trim pads are clipped to door inner panels, which are sealed with water deflectors. On removal of trim pads and water deflectors, door mechanisms can be reached.

The water deflector consists of a paper sheet waterproofed on one side by a coating of polythene. Its object is to prevent the entry of water and dust into the door. Any water percolating past the inner door panel is deflected downwards between the panel and the deflector and back into the door through holes in the panel, then drains through slots in the bottom of the door. These slots are masked on the underside by rubber seals to prevent the entry of dust into the door. The trim pad attachment holes in the inner panel are sealed by the trim panel attaching clips, the entire assembly thus being made waterproof.

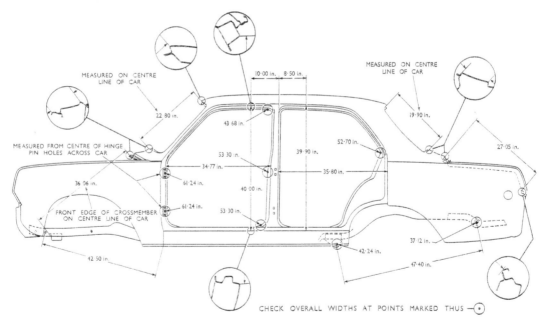

PRINCIPAL BODY DIMENSIONS—NOMINAL

37

VAUXHALL VICTOR 101 AND VX4/90

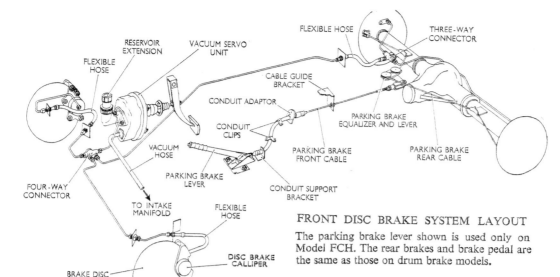

FRONT DISC BRAKE SYSTEM LAYOUT

The parking brake lever shown is used only on Model FCH. The rear brakes and brake pedal are the same as those on drum brake models.

fluid back to reservoir during next operation. Press each piston back into calliper by applying finger pressure to pads. Remove spring clips from pad retaining pins and withdraw pins. Lift friction pads and anti-squeal shims out of calliper. (N.B. Do not press pedal while pads removed). Install new pads and anti-squeal shims in calliper, ensuring that arrow-cut in each shim points in direction of forward rotation of disc, and insert pins and clips. Depress pedal several times to reposition pistons and top up cylinder extension with correct fluid to within 0·30 in. from top.

Checking brake discs for run-out.—Excessive

SECTIONED VIEW OF MASTER CYLINDER

run-out of a disc will push the calliper pistons back into their bores. This will in turn result in increased brake pedal travel upon brake application. Check for run-out as follows: Remove the road wheels. Tighten the hub nut to eliminate all end-float in the bearings so that it is possible to ensure accuracy in checking.

Mount a dial gauge on to the calliper so that the gauge registers on the disc 0·70 in. from the periphery. Now rotate the hub and disc and record any run-out. If it is not within the specified limits, the disc must be renewed. Re-adjust the hub bearings.

CLUTCH

Borg and Beck, Type 8A6 comprising disc, pressure plate and cover. Disc has riveted facings and splined hub, spring loaded by damper springs. Pressure plate thickness, minimum after refacing, 0·465 in. Thrust spring load at 1·56 in., 180-190 lb. Release lever height 1·805–1·825 in. using plate 0·284 : 0·286 in. thick; lever heights must be same within 0·015 in. Tightening torques; clutch to flywheel bolts, 14 lb/ft., flywheel bolts, 48 lb/ft., pedal setscrew (non-tapered type) 18 lb/ft.

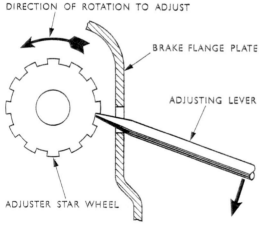

REAR BRAKE ADJUSTER STAR WHEEL (INTERMEDIATE LINK)

Showing the method of rotating the adjuster through the slot in the brake flange plate.

VAUXHALL VICTOR 101 AND VX4/90

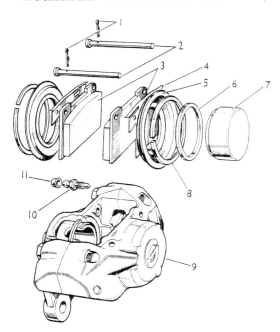

BRAKE CALLIPER ASSEMBLY

The calliper and one piston are part sectioned to show the location of the fluid seal

1. Spring clips
2. Pad retaining pins
3. Friction pads
4. Anti-squeal shim
5. Dust cover
6. Fluid seal
7. Piston
8. Spring ring
9. Calliper
10. Bleed screw
11. Dust cap

ADJUSTMENT.—Fork free travel must be kept to a dimension of 0·10 in. between the nut and the fork.

REMOVAL.—Remove gearbox and detach release bearing from clutch fork. Unscrew clutch cover attaching bolts evenly and remove clutch assembly and disc. Mark clutch cover and pressure plate for reassembly. Bolt assembly to a clutch jig and unscrew eye bolt nuts. Release assembly from jig. Remove cover and components assembled to pressure plate. Remove anti-rattle springs from cover.

COOLING SYSTEM

By pressurised system, incorporating a water pump, fan, thermostat and radiator. There are two drain taps. Water pump is belt driven, centrifugal. Thermostat is capsule type, and radiator has copper film type cooling element. Pressure vent type filler cap creates the pressurising and raises boiling point of coolant.

WATER PUMP.—Note that water thrower on rear end of bearing shaft was deleted on later models.

Removal of Pump.—Drain system, disconnect hose/s from pump, remove fan, distance piece and pulley. Remove securing bolts and nut and lift away pump. If required, remove rotor, using three-legged drag, withdraw and discard seal. On installation, grease rear face of seal and round body. Press rotor on, with 0·03–0·06 in. clearance from pump body. Use new gasket with sealing compound on both sides for reassembly.

Cooling system capacity 11¾ Imp. pints, except FCH, which has 13¾ pints. Radiator leak test pressure 7–10 lb/sq. in. Filler cap pressure-valve opening pressure 7 lb/sq. in. Fan belt should depress 0·5 in. midway between fan and generator pulleys under load of 8–10 lb. if the correct degree of tension is obtained.

ELECTRICAL SYSTEM

12-volt positive earth, current-voltage control. Battery, Exide 6VTMZ9L or Lucas BHN9A (38 amp. hr.) or Exide 6XNMZ9AL (54 amp. hr.) Voltage controller, Lucas RB340, 12 v.

Charging System.—Lucas generator, C40 or C40/1, 22 amps., 2250 r.p.m. at 13·5 volts, or heavy duty Lucas C40L, 25 amps, 2275 r.p.m. at 13·5 volts.

Starting System.—Lucas M.35 G/1 starter, Lucas 2St solenoid switch.

Lighting System.—Either sealed beam or prefocus headlamps. Flasher lamps with automatic cancelling. Thermal circuit breaker.

ENGINE

GENERAL.—The FC 30 unit and the higher powered FC 31 are both 97·4 cu. in. (1,594 c.c.) four-cylinder over-square units with pushrod operated valves. On the FC 30 at Eng. No. FC/100111 the intake ports on the head were enlarged

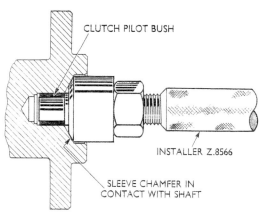

INSTALLING A CLUTCH PILOT BUSH WITH INSTALLER

The pilot of the installer must project through the bush with the nut contacting the sleeve.

39

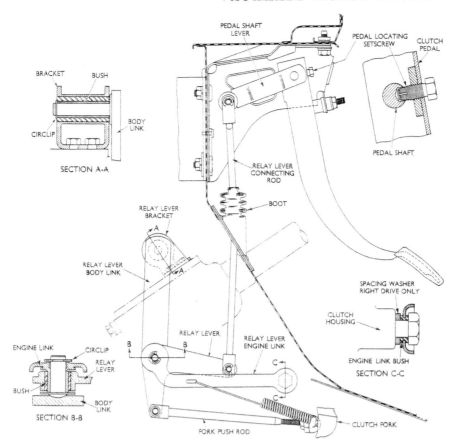

CLUTCH RELAY LINKAGE. THE PEDAL LOCATING SETSCREW ON EARLIER MODELS HAD A TAPERED SHANK.

to match a new manifold, and a new carburetter and air cleaner were introduced.

ENGINE REMOVAL.—Drain oil, drain cooling system and remove radiator. Disconnect heater hoses, brake servo hose and screen washer tube. Remove air cleaner and carburetter controls. On early right-drive models remove throttle cross-shaft. Disconnect exhaust pipe, fuel pump feed-hose, oil gauge hose, wiring harness, starter cable, earth strap etc.

Remove front mounting engine-attachment bolts. To give clearance for inclined removal of unit, raise and support the front of the car. Remove propeller shaft and insert a spare sliding sleeve in the gearbox rear cover to prevent any possibility of oil drainage.

Disconnect speedo. cable. On three-speed, take off cross-shaft coupling from striking lever shaft and remove stay-rod bracket. On four-speed, remove lever boot. Unscrew lever pivot bolt nut and withdraw bolt from carrier. Retain locking ball and washer at end of bolt and lift out lever spring and retainer.

Take off clutch relay engine link from clutch housing. On right-drive a spacing washer is installed behind link. Disconnect pushrod from clutch fork. Support engine with a sling hooked to lifting plate and rear of exhaust manifold. Remove engine rear mounting cross-member. With engine raised at front, to give correct angle for removal, use floor jack or trolley to support the rear end of gearbox to prevent any possible damage to the rear cover sleeve.

Notes on Reassembly and Installation.—Ensure that correct crankshaft installed in FC 31 engine, identified by Part No. 6380632 or 6393978. The crankshaft having the latter number is an earlier type with clutch pilot bearing.

Using a dial gauge, check crankshaft end-float by moving shaft to extreme forward and rear positions. Oversize thrust washers supplied for excessive float. Projection of main bearing oil-seal felts must be 0·06 in. when sump fitted. On FC 31 unit, fit a new sealing washer behind elbow and elbow attaching nut when fitting oil pump delivery pipe and elbow assembly.

On installation of engine, adjust clutch-fork free travel. On FC 31, check carburetter choke-flaps.

VAUXHALL VICTOR 101 AND VX4/90

These should open and close when operated. Adjust fan-belt tension. Check timings and timing chain tension.

CAMSHAFT AND BEARINGS.—Shaft is in three bearings and driven by duplex roller chain. Thrust plate bolted to crankcase controls camshaft end-float. Chain tensioner has manual adjustment.

To remove camshaft, take off radiator, valve tappets, timing chain and wheels, oil pump, fuel pump and thrust plate. Withdraw shaft. On replacement, lubricate, and assemble a gasket to thrust plate. Align valve timing marks on timing wheels. When installing rocker gear, be sure end brackets on FC 31 are engaged on locating dowels. Re-check valve clearances with warm engine.

CRANKSHAFT AND BEARINGS.—Three-bearing crankshaft, end-float controlled by thrust washers each side of centre main. Semi-circular oil seals at rear end and spring-loaded seal at front. Solid skirt pistons with offset pins, fully floating.

Crankshaft removal conventional, after taking engine-gearbox unit out and removing flywheel and clutch housing. Mark main bearing caps and remove caps and bearings, using slide hammer D 1129 and remover SE 673. Lift out shaft and remove bearings.

A reground shaft must not be used on FC 31 unless main journal and pin fillets have been re-rolled to original specification. Maximum undersize 0·010 in.

CYLINDER HEAD.—On FC 30, a standard high-compression head marked H and an optional low compression head marked L are available. Valves work in pressed-in guides. On FC 31 valves are inclined and non-replaceable seat inserts are cast into head. Oil seals on stems of inlets. Rockers on hollow shaft in brackets bolted to head. Front and rear brackets on FC 31 located by dowels for alignment.

Cylinder Head Removal.—Drain cooling system, remove rocker gear, withdraw manifolds. Remove bolts attaching thermostat housing and lifting plate to head, take out plugs, ignition control pipe, temp.

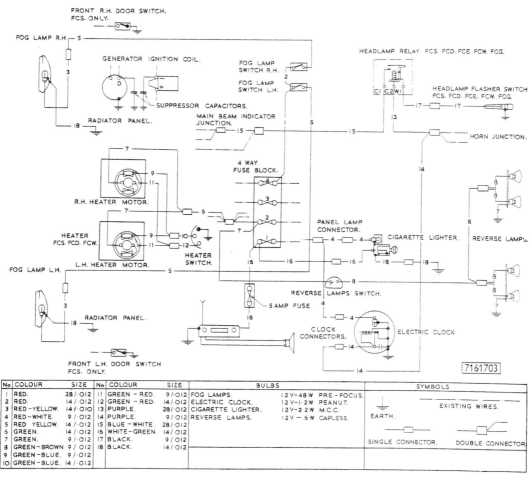

ACCESSORY WIRING DIAGRAM

gauge wire. Remove pushrod cover, disconnect generator brace from head, remove head nuts, also washers on FC 31. Lift head and discard gasket.

On installation, check that rocker gear oil feed in block and head are free from obstruction. On FC 31 avoid damaging head face with studs. Plain washers to be assembled below head attaching nuts. Tighten nuts to 73 lb/ft. (dry).

LUBRICATION.—Pump driven from camshaft by skew gears, one of which is riveted to pump driving impeller spindle. Spindle drilled to conduct oil under pressure up to two radial metering holes which discharge oil through slot in upper face of pump body for lubricating skew gears. Spring-loaded relief valve. On FC 30 a pipe connects pump delivery port to main oil gallery. FC 31 has the pump delivery port connected by pipe and elbow to full-flow oil filter.

On FC 30, by-pass filter with detachable element bolted to crankcase. Flow controlled by metering hole. Full flow type on FC 31 has detachable element and by-pass valve for flow to main gallery if choked.

Warning light for oil check on facia. Excess pressure or loss of pressure shown by repeated switch failure and continuous light respectively.

Sump Removal.—Remove front suspension cross brace, clutch housing bottom cover plate and front cover.

Sump capacity: 7½ Imp. pints (dry engine), 6 Imp. pints (refill)

PISTONS, RINGS AND CONNECTING RODS. Each connecting rod and cap is machined together in a non-interchangeable pair identified by pairing numbers on one side of rod and cap.

For removal of piston pin, take off circlips, heat piston in water to 48°C and push out pin, and reverse procedure for installation. Disassembly

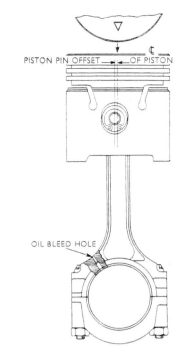

CORRECT ASSEMBLY OF PISTON TO CONNECTING ROD
The front of the piston is identified by an arrow head cast in the piston.

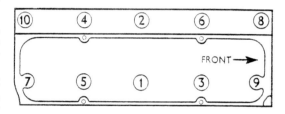

CYLINDER HEAD NUT TIGHTENING SEQUENCE

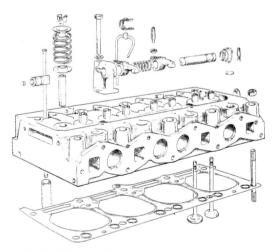

CYLINDER HEAD COMPONENTS—FC 30 ENGINE

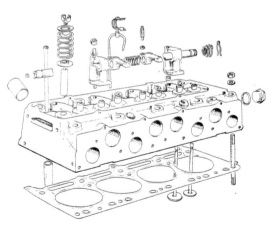

CYLINDER HEAD COMPONENTS—FC 31 ENGINE

and assembly of pistons and rings is carried out in the normal manner. Front of piston is identified by an arrow head in crown.

ENGINE DATA

General

Bore	3·125 in.
Stroke	3·0 in.
Capacity	92 cu. in.
Compression ratio:	
Standard FC 30	8·5 : 1
Optional FC 30	7·0 : 1
Standard FC 31	9·3 : 1
Clutch to flywheel bolts	14 lb/ft. (dry)
Oil filter bolt	10 lb/ft. (dry)
Firing order	1-3-4-2
Oil pressure, hot	35–45 lb/sq. in. at 3,000 r.p.m.

Bearings

Crankshaft diameters:	
Main journal:	
Front, standard	2·1198–2·1208 in.
Front, grade J, FC 30	2·1098–2·1108 in.
Centre, standard FC 31	2·1200–2·1205 in.
Centre, standard FC 30	2·1203–2·1208 in.
Centre, grade J, FC 30	2·1103–2·1108 in.
Rear, standard	2·1201–2·1206 in.
Rear, grade J, FC 30	2·1101–2·1106 in.
Crankpin:	
Standard	1·8725–1·8735 in.
Grade P, FC 30	1·8625–1·8635 in.
Camshaft journal diameters:	
Front	1·9132–1·9137 in.
Centre	1·7570–1·7575 in.
Rear	1·7258–1·7263 in.
Diametral clearances:	
Main bearings:	
Front	0·0005–0·0024 in.
Centre, FC 30	0·0005–0·0019 in.
Centre FC 31	0·0008–0·0022 in.
Rear	0·0007–0·0021 in.
Big-end bearings	0·0005–0·0025 in.
Camshaft bearings:	
Front	0·0063 in.
Centre	0·0065 in.
Rear	0·0067 in.
End float:	
Crankshaft	0·002–0·012 in.
Camshaft	0·002–0·004 in.

Pistons

Oversizes	0·005, 0·020, 0·040 in.
Clearance in bore	0·0007–0·0012 in.
Ring gaps	0·08–0·022 in.
Ring clearance in groove:	
Top, compression	0·0015–0·0035 in.
Centre, compression	0·0010–0·0030 in.
Scraper	0·0017–0·0037 in.

Torque wrench settings

Con-rod nuts	22 lb/ft. (oiled)
Main bearing bolts	58 lb/ft. (oiled)
Flywheel bolts	48 lb/ft. (dry)
Rocker bracket bolts or nuts	42 lb/ft. (dry)
Cylinder head nuts	73 lb/ft. (dry)

Valves

Clearance, hot	0·013 in.
Timing	Inlet valve maximum opening point 109° after T.D.C. (37 teeth of flywheel ring gear)
Face angle in cylinder head	45°
on valve	44°
Spring free length:	
Inlet	1·78 in.
Exhaust	1·86 in.
Spring load at 1·52 in.:	
Inlet	34–55 lb.
Exhaust	54–60 lb.
Valve stem diameter:	
Inlet	0·3102–0·3110 in.
Exhaust	0·3096–0·3103 in.
Stem clearance:	
Inlet	0·005 in.
Exhaust	0·004 in.

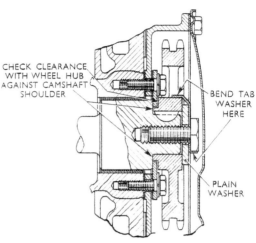

METHOD OF ATTACHING CAMSHAFT TIMING WHEEL

VALVES

Valve Clearance Adjustment.—Except for initial adjustment after rocker gear dismantling, clearance must be checked with engine at normal temperature and running at idling speed. Use screwdriver D 1031 and spanner.

Timing.—Normally by aligning marks on timing wheels, but can be checked without removing timing cover as follows:

Remove clutch housing bottom cover, mark 37th tooth from TDC (U/C mark on flywheel) counting anti-clockwise as from front. Detach timing aperture plug and mount dial gauge over No. 1 intake valve so that gauge plunger contacts valve spring cap. Turn engine clockwise until valve is fully open; mark on flywheel should be in line with notch in timing aperture.

Rocker Gear.—If there is evidence of inadequate lubrication rotate engine and check for oil flow from oil feed drilling in cylinder head. Clean rocker-shaft oil pipe and check the crimped end. When dismantling rocker gear on FC 31, take care that dowels for end brackets not dislodged from studs, or they may fall down pushrod chamber.

FRONT AXLE AND FRONT SUSPENSION

FRONT SUSPENSION DATA

(With car at kerb weight, i.e. unladen with fuel tank full)

Toe-in	0·12–0·24 in.
Camber angle	$\frac{1}{2}°–1\frac{3}{4}°$
Steering pivot inclination	$5\frac{1}{4}°–6\frac{3}{4}°$
Castor angle FCS/D/E	$\frac{1}{4}°–3\frac{1}{4}°$
With increased ground clearance (Code 307)	0°–3°
FCH	$\frac{1}{2}°–3\frac{1}{4}°$
With Code 307	0°–3$\frac{1}{2}$°
FCG	0°–3°
With Code 307	$\frac{1}{4}°–3\frac{1}{4}°$
FCW	0°–3°
With Code 307	1°–3$\frac{1}{4}$°
Front end standing height	8·10–10·50 in. from floor to centre of lower fulcrum shaft

The independent front suspension is mounted on body and incorporates coil springs with long and short arms, telescopic dampers and a front stabiliser. Front hubs have taper rollers. Suspension arms are rubber mounted on fulcrum shafts shimmed to provide adjustment for castor and camber angles.

Each steering knuckle is carried on spring-

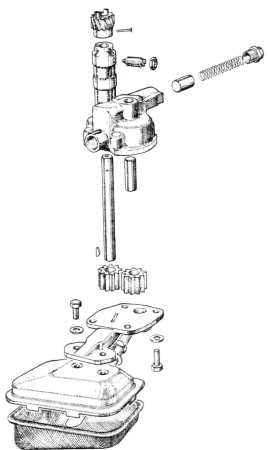

OIL PUMP COMPONENTS

loaded ball joint in outer end of upper arm and a pendant ball joint in lower arm. Pendant joint carries loads in tension only. Upper end of spring is rubber insulated from its seat on body. Spring free length on driver's side is greater than on passenger's.

ADJUSTMENTS.—Castor angle adjustment should be carried out before adjusting camber. Two methods for former are by slotted shims behind upper fulcrum shaft and by shims between lower fulcrum shaft bush housings and suspension arm support. Initial adjustment at upper fulcrum shaft. If sufficient correction unobtainable, make adjustment at lower fulcrum shaft.

Adjustment of camber angle and steering pivot inclination is effected by varying the number of two-hole shims behind the upper fulcrum shaft. One shim will alter the angles by $\frac{1}{4}°$. Total of shims must not exceed six on either bolt, including camber shims.

Regarding front hub bearing adjustment, note that it is possible to rock front wheel about 0·20 in. due to clearance in lower arm joint. This can be

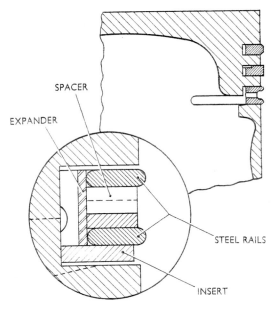

PISTON RING LOCATIONS

The inset shows the special service Vauxhall oil control ring components.

VAUXHALL VICTOR 101 AND VX4/90

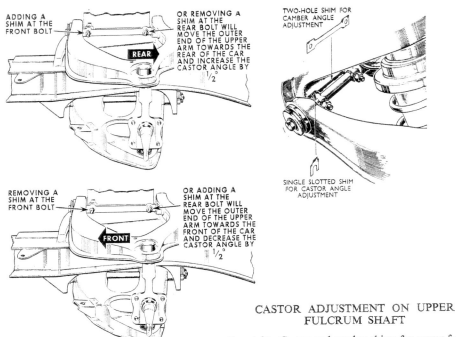

CASTOR ADJUSTMENT ON UPPER FULCRUM SHAFT

Top right: Castor and camber shims for upper fulcrum shaft. Shim adjustment at the rear bolt also affects camber.

eliminated for checking by levering with a bar of adequate strength against the lock stop bracket and steering arms.

REMOVING SUSPENSION UPPER ARMS.— Remove front spring, disconnect upper ball joint from knuckle, move brake and knuckle to one side and support so that hose need not be disconnected. Remove nuts and take off arm and shaft assembly, noting position and number of adjusting shims. Note that renewal of fulcrum shaft bushes not practicable and arm assembly must be renewed. After installation check geometry. Lubricate joint with enough grease to fill rubber boot, checking by light finger pressure on latter.

REMOVING SUSPENSION LOWER ARMS.— Remove front spring and take off spring compressor. If both arms to be removed other spring must be taken off at this stage. Remove nuts and bolts securing fulcrum shaft bush housings to arm support and withdraw lower arms. Note shimming. Remove nuts and washers from shaft and withdraw bushes and housings. Remove rubber boot.

Check ball joint for roughness when ball is pulled hard against seating. Check ball vertical clearance with dial gauge. Renew if clearance exceeds 0·085 in.

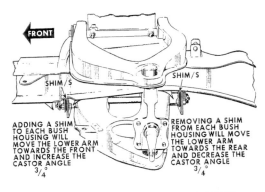

CASTOR ADJUSTMENT ON LOWER FULCRUM SHAFT

The number of shims installed on the front and rear housings of one side must be equal.

FUEL SUPPLY SYSTEM

The single carburetter on FC 30 and twins on FC 31 are supplied from tank by a diaphragm-type pump. The air cleaner has either a paper or a polyurethane foam element. Fuel pump is AC, FG type, carburetters are Zenith 341V.

On the FC 30 engine at No. 100111, modifications to the carburetter, air cleaner and intake manifold became effective. The new carburetter has an inner choke tube in addition to a larger outer choke tube and revised jet settings. A new air cleaner, using the paper element only, provides increased air flow. Intake manifold ports are larger for improved mixture flow and new gaskets and collars are used.

VAUXHALL VICTOR 101 AND VX4/90

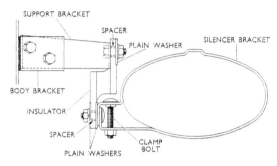

CYLINDER BLOCK AND CRANKCASE COMPONENTS

SILENCER MOUNTING DETAILS
Note that the insulator has two detachable spacers.

GEARBOX

GENERAL.—The three-speed and four-speed transmissions are similar in basic design and have synchromesh on all forward speeds. The synchromesh mechanism on the four-speed incorporates two clutch and clutch-hub assemblies. Steering column shift is used for the three-speed and on the four-speed box gear selection is by a central floor-type lever. Combined oil level and filler plug on left-hand side of transmission casing; periodic draining and refilling is not required. Oil level should be at bottom of filler hole. SAE 90 oil is used, and SAE 80 for below-zero temperatures overseas.

TROUBLE DIAGNOSIS

Difficulty in Engaging Gears.—Ensure that clutch pedal and fork are correctly adjusted. Check gear shift control. Trouble may be due to worn or incorrectly adjusted linkage on three-speed.

Faulty Synchromesh Action.—Lack of frictional grip between synchronising ring and cone due to wear or damage; weak, broken or displaced sliding key springs in respective clutch hub; worn or damaged teeth on ring. In all cases transmission must be dismantled for rectification of faults in the synchro-mesh mechanism.

Gear Hop-out.—On three-speed this can be due to incorrectly adjusted shift linkage, preventing full engagement. In the case of top speed this may be due to slackness of the bolts securing the transmission to the housing, foreign matter between front face and clutch housing, or slackness in main drive pinion bearing.

Other points which can cause hop-out of any speeds are: Weak or broken locking-ball springs; excessive slackness between a clutch and hub; wear or damage at ends of clutch internal splines and on the engagement teeth of the appropriate mainshaft gear or main drive pinion. This condition will prevent satisfactory operation of anti-jump-out characteristics of keystone contour on splines and teeth; slackness in bearings and undue float of mainshaft.

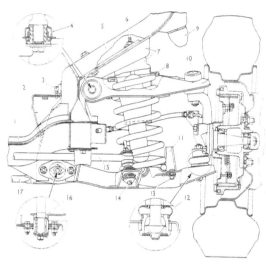

GENERAL ARRANGEMENT OF FRONT SUSPENSION—LEFT-HAND SIDE SHOWN

The inset (12) shows a lower arm ball joint in the normal laden condition. Note that a vertical clearance exists in the joint. This results in slackness of the joint when the wheel is jacked off the ground.

1. Front crossmember
2. Engine mounting bracket
3. Upper arm mounting bolt and locking rod
4. Upper fulcrum shaft rubber mounting
5. Front wheelhouse brace
6. Shock absorber upper securing stud
7. Shock absorber housing and spring seat
8. Front spring insulator
9. Bump stop
10. Upper arm ball joint
11. Steering lock stop
12. Lower arm ball joint
13. Shock absorber lower housing bracket
14. Stabiliser link bolt
15. Stabiliser shaft
16. Lower fulcrum shaft rubber mounting
17. Front suspension cross brace

VAUXHALL VICTOR 101 AND VX4/90

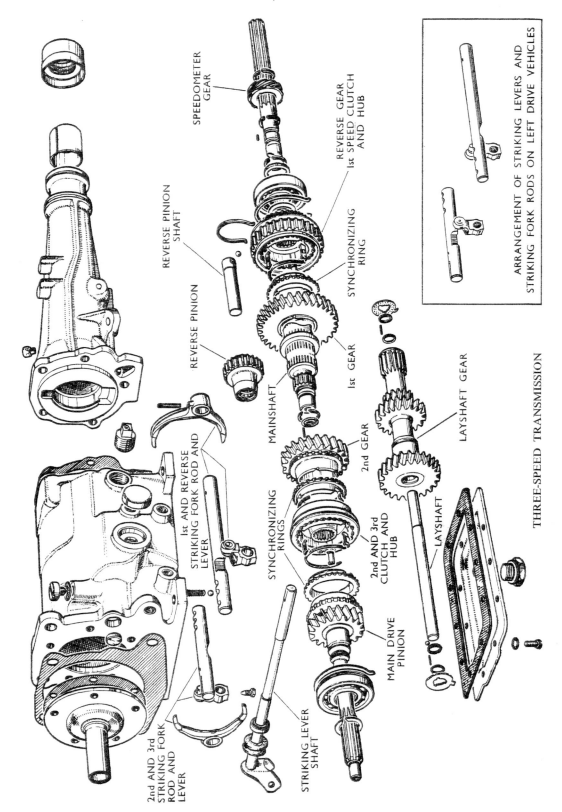

THREE-SPEED TRANSMISSION

VAUXHALL VICTOR 101 AND VX4/90

Speedometer driven gear, rear cover and striking lever shaft all have oil seals, drifts being used for removal and replacement of seals, which must be lubricated before it is fitted. The striking lever shaft seal must be fitted with the lip towards the inside of transmission casing thus ensuring satisfactory operation.

GEARBOX OVERHAUL

Removal.—On four-speed, remove gear shift lever. Drain oil. On three-speed, disconnect change-speed cross-shaft coupling from striking lever shaft and remove stay-rod bracket on side of casing. Remove prop-shaft and disconnect speedometer cable. Support engine and remove nut and washers securing engine rear mounting to cross-member and four bolts securing cross-member to under-body member. Remove clutch housing bottom cover. Remove bolts securing transmission to clutch housing and withdraw transmission.

Dismantling.—On four-speed, remove shift linkage. Secure a suitable support plate to gearbox and mount assembly in a vice. Remove rear mounting, speedometer gear, bottom cover, and on four-speed boxes, the reverse stop housing. Remove bolts securing rear cover to casing and rotate cover to expose rear end of layshaft. With a brass drift, drive out layshaft from rear to front, retaining locking ball at front end of shaft. Lift out layshaft gear and discard needle rollers and two thrust washers. Remove setscrews securing striking levers to shaft and withdraw shaft and levers.

Remove retaining screws and withdraw striking fork locking balls and springs. Drive striking fork retaining pins through the forks sufficiently to release the forks on the rods. On three-speed, engage reverse to support rear of rod when driving out first and reverse fork retaining pin. Do not drive out pins completely as they may jam on casing. With brass drift, drive out striking fork rods from rear to front. The end covers will be driven out by the fork rods. Remove striking forks, withdraw reverse pinion shaft and lift away pinion. Remove bolts securing front cover and withdraw main drive pinion, bearing and cover assembly. Take out mainshaft assembly and rear cover and drive the striking lever shaft oil seal out of the casing.

Main Drive Pinion.—Remove needle rollers from main drive pinion counterbore, expand pinion bearing circlip in front cover and withdraw pinion and bearing assembly by tapping end of shaft on a lead block. Remove circlip from pinion, remove circlip from front cover and assemble it to groove in bearing outer race. Support circlip on a tube and press out pinion. Remove circlip.

Mainshaft and Rear Cover.—Remove mainshaft rear bearing circlip from rear cover and press mainshaft assembly out of cover, which may have to be warmed. On four-speed, mark first and second-speed clutch hub for identity on reassembly. Remove rear of two circlips locating speedometer gear, press off and retain key. Remove other circlip. Remove mainshaft rear bearing circlip and thrust washer.

On three-speed, dismantle mainshaft gear assembly by supporting front face of mainshaft first-speed gear on bed of a press and press mainshaft out of first-speed clutch, reverse gear hub and mainshaft rear bearing. Withdraw first-speed clutch and reverse gear from clutch hub and remove keys and springs from hub. Take the second and third-speed hub circlip off the front end of mainshaft. Support rear face of mainshaft second-speed gear on bed of press and press shaft out of second and third-speed hub. Withdraw the clutch from the hub and take off the keys and springs.

On four-speed, dismantle mainshaft assembly by removing third and fourth hub circlip from front end. Support rear face of third gear on bed of press and press out shaft. Withdraw clutch from hub and remove keys and springs. Support front face of second gear on bed of press and press shaft out of hub, first-gear sleeve and mainshaft rear bearing. Withdraw clutch from hub and take off keys and springs.

Bottom Cover—Four-speed.—Remove retaining screw, withdraw striking fork rod locking-ball and spring. Remove expansion plug from each end of striking fork rod bore. Move rod until shift fork retaining pin is in line with drain plug hole and drive out pin. Move rod until striking fork retaining pin is in line with drain plug hole. Support rear end of rod, drive out pin and remove rod and forks.

Reassembly of Gearbox.—Always include the following among parts to be renewed: Front cover bolt copper washers, circlips, sliding key springs, striking fork pins and striking rod end covers.

Longitudinal location of the mainshaft is controlled by the ball bearing and it is imperative that it be correctly located. Where necessary, shims are interposed between rear abutment face of first and reverse hub and the bearing on three-speed and between mainshaft thrust washer and bearing on four-speed. Gauge Z 8518 is used for this operation.

Needle rollers are positioned with petroleum jelly, but do not use an excess for fear of choking oilways.

Other points: On top speed forks, the legs are of equal length. On three-speed boxes, engage reverse to support rear of rod when installing first and reverse fork retaining pin. Layshaft thrust washers are not interchangeable. The front washer has a flat on the periphery.

INSTALLATION.—Inject ⅓ pint transmission oil through end of rear cover to provide initial lubrication for speedometer gears and rear cover bush. Do not allow weight of gearbox to hang on main drive pinion after it has entered hub of clutch disc.

PROPELLER SHAFT AND UNIVERSAL JOINTS.—Two makes of propeller shaft are used, i.e. Hardy Spicer and BRD, and are identified by the name cast on the yoke. In both cases the tubular shaft incorporates two universal joints of the trunnion and needle roller bearing type. The sleeve of the front universal is splined internally to engage the rear end of the transmission mainshaft and is supported in the transmission rear cover bush.

The sleeve is free to move longitudinally on the mainshaft and in the bush to compensate for movement of the rear axle. An oil seal in the transmission rear cover operates directly on the sliding sleeve. The universal joint trunnions are lubricated on initial assembly and need no routine maintenance.

The universals have 34 needle rollers in each bearing. The diameter of the sliding sleeve is 1·3735–1·3750 in.

IGNITION
TUNE-UP DATA

Firing order	1-3-4-2
Ignition timing	Contacts open 9° before t.d.c. with steel ball in line with notch in clutch housing aperture.
Contact breaker gap	New, 0·021–0·023 in. Service, 0·019–0·021 in.
Sparking plugs	AC 43 (FC 30) AC 44XL (FC 31)
Plug gap	0·028–0·032 in.
Vacuum advance (max.)	11° (crankshaft)
Centrifugal advance (max.):	
FC 30 engine	33° (crankshaft)
FC 31 engine	30° (crankshaft)
Coil	Delco-Remy, oil-filled
Distributor	Delco-Remy, D202

REAR AXLE AND REAR SUSPENSION

REAR AXLE.—There are two types of rear axle—that with the standard differential and that with the super-traction differential, the latter being a special limited-slip type.

The semi-floating rear axle incorporates a hypoid final drive with overhung pinion. On the standard axle, lateral location of the assembly and pre-load of the bearings is controlled by spacers between bearing outer races and axle housing. The hypoid pinion is mounted in the housing in two pre-loaded taper roller bearings. A compressible spacer between front and rear bearing inner races provides a clamping force on the universal joint coupling-flange nut. Shims between rear bearing outer race and axle housing locate the pinion in relationship to the hypoid gear.

The flanged type axle shafts are carried in

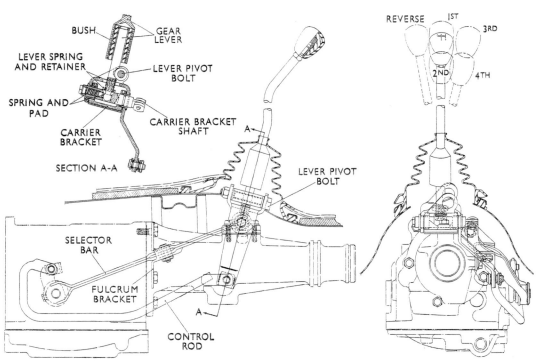

GENERAL LAYOUT OF FOUR-SPEED GEAR SHIFT LINKAGE

VAUXHALL VICTOR 101 AND VX4/90

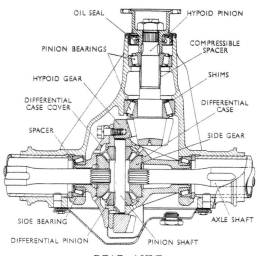

REAR AXLE

sealed ball bearings located by retaining plates which, with the brake flange plates, are bolted to the flanges on the housing.

On all models except FCW and FCG, the axle shaft bearing embodies a lip-type oil seal, and in addition has an oil sealing ring in the outer race to prevent oil leakage between the bearing and the axle housing. A pressed-on flanged ring retains the bearing on the shaft. On the models mentioned, the shaft bearings are larger and the seal operates on a ground collar pressed on to the shaft.

The hypoid gears need the recommended hypoid lubricants. The combined oil level and filler plug is located on the axle housing rear cover. Periodic draining and refilling of the rear axle unit is not required.

AXLE SHAFT REMOVAL.—Remove road wheel and release brake. Take off bolts securing brake drum to axle-shaft flange and withdraw drum. Take off nuts securing axle-shaft bearing retaining plate and withdraw shaft. On FCW and FCG, withdraw shaft enough to insert axle-shaft guide Z8420, then complete removal of shaft. Do not allow splines to foul oil seal.

Renewing Axle-shaft Bearing and Oil Seal Assembly.—On all models except FCW and FCG the bearing incorporates an oil seal. To renew the bearing except on those models slacken the bearing retaining ring by nicking with a chisel. On FCW and FCG slacken oil seal collar and bearing ring in a similar manner. Press shaft out of bearing, using removal plate Z8461 and (except FCW/FCG) inserts Z8475.

With retainer plate assembled to shaft, press on new bearing, so that oil seal is facing shaft splines (except FCW/FCG). Press bearing home against shaft shoulder.

Except FCW/FCG, position new retaining ring squarely on shaft bearing land with ring collar facing bearing. Do not heat ring. Support end face of ring boss on installer Z8553 and press shaft through ring until collar firm against inner race. On FCW/FCG heat a new ring on hotplate to dark blue. Quickly place ring in contact with bearing using pliers and slide installer SE 525 over shaft into contact with ring and leave in position until ring is cool. Press oil seal collar home with external chamfered end towards splined end of shaft.

On FCW/FCG, to renew oil seal (not incorporated in bearing) withdraw using seal remover D 1134. Locate new seal so that lip of seal faces inwards. Drive seal into housing until dimension from outer face of seal casing to outer face of axle housing flange is 1·20 in.

Installing Axle Shaft.—Check that oil drain hole in brake flange plate is clear. Put a new gasket in position on the flange plate so that the hole coincides with the hole in the plate. On all models except FCW/FCG, assemble a new outer oil seal to the groove in the bearing outer race. Lubricate

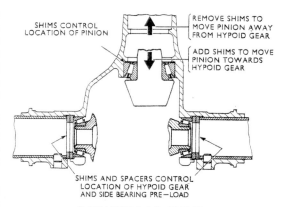

LOCATION OF SHIMS

Showing the shims interposed between the pinion rear bearing outer race and housing and between the differential side bearing spacers.

the outer oil seal and the axle-shaft bearing housing bore to facilitate entry of the seal.

On FCW/FCG coat oil seal in housing with oil. Coat shaft with oil. Recharge axle tube if necessary with ¼ pint of oil. On FCW/FCG it is essential that axle-shaft guide is used, otherwise seal will be damaged.

After inserting shaft, locate retainer plate so that oil-drain recess lines up with drain hole in brake plate. Check oil level.

Renewing Pinion Oil Seal.—Raise car. Disconnect propeller shaft at rear. Withdraw shaft and insert a spare sliding sleeve in transmission rear cover to prevent oil loss. Tap back staking on pinion nut and remove. Withdraw universal joint

VAUXHALL VICTOR 101 AND VX4/90

coupling flange. Cut through pinion seal case with small chisel and prise from housing. With $\frac{3}{16}$ in. round file, cut a slot opposite existing slot in end of shaft. Place new seal with lip inwards. Check seal land for burrs. Smear seal with oil and install joint flange. Fit pinion nut and lock by staking into new slot.

DISMANTLING REAR AXLE.—The main procedure is normal, but it should be noted that the side bearing caps are not interchangeable, the right-hand one being marked. If the pinion bearings are to be used again, the pinion must be pressed from the axle housing to avoid damage. Pinion bearing outer races are removed and installed with listed tools.

ASSEMBLING DIFFERENTIAL AND HYPOID GEAR.—Dip parts in oil. Place a differential side gear in the case. Locate the two differential pinions in position, insert pinion shaft opposite dowel and tap home so that slot in end of shaft engages the dowel.

Place remaining side gear in position and assemble cover to case, engaging dowel in case with hole in cover. Install hypoid gear on case register by making up a pair of guide studs, then warming the gear on a hotplate. Quickly screw studs into two opposite bolt holes in gear, locate gear and assemble bolts with new lock-washers. Tighten to 38 lb/ft. (clean dry threads).

Lateral location of differential and hypoid gear, and pre-load of side bearings, are controlled in service by spacers and shims, which in production are from 0·200 to 0·243 in., but in service are in two grades of spacer—0·100–0·101—and one grade of shim 0·003 in. thick. With two spacers and one shim thickness, the whole range from 0·200 in. upwards can be covered in steps of 0·001 in. by using two spacers and the necessary shims. The 0·100 spacer has a localised chamfer ground on the face.

The differential assembly and hypoid gear, with side bearings, are replaced in the normal manner and adjusted by means of the spacers and shims for pre-load, which is 1 lb. for used bearings and 2½–3 lb. for new ones.

After installation in the axle housing, mount a dial gauge on the housing and check for run-out on the back face of the hypoid gear. It must not exceed 0·001 in. (mating face), 0·002 in. (rear face). Hypoid gear backlash with pinion is 0·006–0·008 in., and is adjusted by the interchanging of shims from one side to the other.

REAR SUSPENSION.—Spring eyes and shackles are rubber bushed and rubber pads insulate axle attachment. Front hangers are welded to underbody members. On left side, rear shackle bushes are in a tube welded in side member. On right side, shackle tube is welded in a box-type bracket below side member, the bracket also serving as a spring stop.

The spring upper insulator retainer is an integral part of the spring seat welded to the axle housing. The spring is located in the spring seat between two rubber insulators by the spring and damper anchor plate which is secured to the seat by four bolts and nuts.

Removing Shackle and Hanger Bushes.—Jack up axle. Detach wheel and damper. Remove nuts from shackle and hanger pins and withdraw shackle plate and pins. Lower axle and remove shackle and spring eye bushes. On installation ensure that shackle pins are towards the right-hand side of the vehicle and hanger pins towards the inside. Do not tighten shackle pin nuts until weight of vehicle is on rear axle.

Rear Spring Checking, Removal and Installation.—If spring weakness suspected, measure vertical distance from top of axle tube to underside of rubber bump stop. (Vehicle unladen, except for full fuel tank.) Standing height should be 9·25–10·25 in.

For removal, take off road wheel, remove nuts and bolts securing spring anchor-plate and swing plate clear of spring. Jack up axle and remove spring insulators. Remove shackle and hanger-pin nuts, withdraw pins and lift away spring. Remove

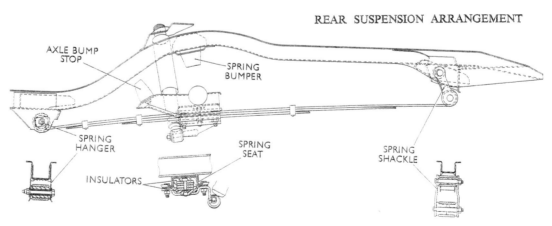

REAR SUSPENSION ARRANGEMENT

rubber bushes from spring eyes.

Installation Notes.—Assemble spring front-eye bush, using a soap solution and install spring with shorter end (measured from centre bolt) towards front. Install shackle pins towards right-hand side of vehicle and hanger pins towards inside. Do not tighten nuts until weight of vehicle is on rear axle. Renew insulators if needed. They are not interchangeable. Anchor-plate bolts must be fully tightened.

SHOCK ABSORBERS

Notes on Dismantling and Installation.—Do not remove upper securing nuts or lower attachment when front wheels are off the floor unless weight of vehicle is taken by suspension lower arm or spring compressor Z 8517 is in place. To gain access to upper nuts on rear shock absorbers on models FCG/FCW, fold back carpet. On other models gain access from boot.

STEERING

Recirculating-ball type gear and three-rod linkage, connecting a drop arm and relay lever to two steering arms. The aluminium case is riveted to the column. A single-start worm is welded to the shaft. Two ball bearings support the worm in the case and steel shims between bottom end-plate gaskets provide bearing adjustment. The upper end of the shaft is supported in a spring-loaded ball bearing.

The worm is engaged by steel balls circulating in the main nut. The drop arm is supported at its outer end by a bush in the casing which also carries an oil seal. The inner end of the shaft rotates direct in the bore of the casing. An adjusting screw is provided in the side cover to control shaft end float.

Steering connecting rods are spring-loaded. Maximum permissible movement on a used joint is 0·06 in. Steering tie-rod may be straightened if slightly bent, but do not heat. Bushes or grommets are easily renewed and are fitted with liquid soap. Correct length of grommet is obtained by the compression created by the bush. Steering drop arm should be to specified dimensions and arm and shaft serrations should be free of wear. Steering relay lever should be tight on its shaft and dimensionally correct.

Load required to rotate relay lever in its housing is 3 lb. Housing bracket bolts and nut securing tie-rod to be tightened to 25 lb/ft.

The steering-shaft bearing is easily renewable after removing steering wheel, bearing spring, etc. After installation, the steering-wheel nut must be tightened to 38 lb/ft.

Renewing Worm and Shaft.—Wear on steering-shaft inner races may result in balls wearing a

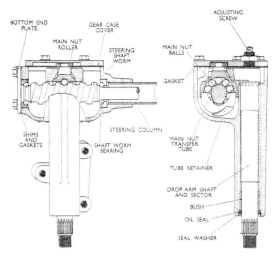

SECTIONED VIEW OF STEERING GEAR

groove in shaft, necessitating renewal of worm and shaft. To renew drop-arm shaft bush, screw a 1 in. tap into outer end of bush, heat case in water, engage a brass drift with inner end of tap and press tap and bush out of case. Locate new bush so that arrow on outside points into case. Press bush in until flush with bottom of oil-seal recess. Arrow indicates open end of oilway. Hone bush to give 0·0010–0·0025 in. clearance.

To renew selector-rod bush, cut a thread in bush using a $\frac{7}{16}$ in. UNF tap, heat case in water, extract bush with nut, bolt, washer and distance piece and press home new bush.

Notes on Reassembly of Steering.—Before installing drop-arm shaft, adjust pre-load of worm bearings by adding or removing shims at bottom end plate. Prior to checking, temporarily fit steering wheel, nut roller, cover and gasket. Check with spring balance tangentially on wheel rim to 2–8 oz.

After fitting shaft, adjust sector and nut engagement as follows: Fit nut roller, cover and gasket, and tighten cover bolts. Set wheel straight ahead. Screw in shaft adjusting screw until it contacts shaft and tighten locknut. Check pre-load to 12–16 oz. through an angle of 30° each side of zero or nil-backlash position.

WHEELS AND TYRES

All models have disc type wheels and tubeless tyres. Four right-hand threaded nuts attach each wheel to bolts pressed into hub flange.

Tyre Sizes.—FCD, FCE, FCH, FCS (standard), 5·60–13 (4-ply); (optional), 5·90–13 (4-ply). FCG, FCW, 5·90–13 (6-ply).

Pressures—Front and Rear.—FCD, FCE, FCS, 24 lb/sq. in.; FCH, 26 lb/sq. in.; FCG, FCW, 24 lb/sq. in. (or 30 lb/sq. in. if combined weight of goods and passengers is 1,000 lb.).

Vauxhall VX4/90 1,594 c.c.

AT A GLANCE: Free-revving but noisy engine, and car too low-geared; good gearbox. Light, positive controls and responsive steering. Road holding greatly improved by radial tyres and optional limited slip differential. Brakes fade in severe use but recover quickly; pedal loads very light. A very eager and lively car with generous space for 5 and their luggage.

BOTH Victor and VX4 90 models of the Vauxhall 101 Series already are seen in large enough numbers for one to forget that the range has been on the market only 18 months; it was, in fact, one of the two most important new models introduced at last year's London Motor Show. The Road Test of the 101 estate car appeared in our 5 March issue, but the VX4 90 has been lost to prolonged television and other commitments, now over at last.

Although the 101 body was entirely new, the mechanical side is little changed, and the power output of 73·8 b.h.p. net is the same as for the previous VX4/90. The new body is quite a bit bigger and more spacious, and there is a slight weight increase of 80 lb, yet performance is fractionally better. At 93 m.p.h., the mean maximum speed is 3 m.p.h. higher, and although most of the acceleration figures are within a second of those timed with the previous car, the difference is on the right side.

Reasons for these gains are a more →

Safety features include a dished steering wheel and a framed interior mirror. The mirror can be dipped at night, but although it has a windscreen support it vibrates badly at high speed

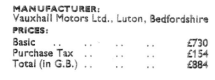

MANUFACTURER:
Vauxhall Motors Ltd., Luton, Bedfordshire
PRICES:
Basic	.. ..	£730
Purchase Tax	.. .. ..	£154
Total (in G.B.)	.. ..	£884

PERFORMANCE SUMMARY
Mean maximum speed ..	93 m.p.h.
Standing start ¼-mile	20·2 sec
0-60 m.p.h.	16·0 sec
30-70 m.p.h. in 3rd	18·5 sec
Overall fuel consumption ..	23·3 m.p.g
Miles per tankful	235

53

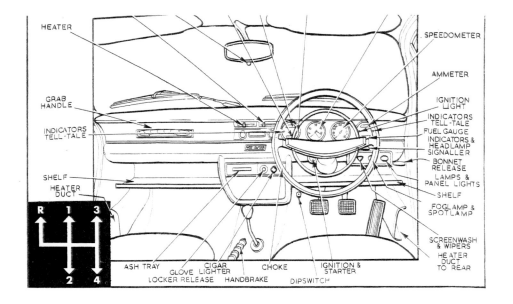

aerodynamic body, and the fact that smaller wheels—13in. instead of 14—are now used, thus lowering the effective gearing of the otherwise unchanged transmission. The road speed at 1,000 r.p.m. in top is down from 18·1 to 17·5 m.p.h., and with the slightly smaller circumference radial-ply tyres offered as an option, the difference is even greater. This goes against today's trend for higher gearing as high-speed roads are extended, and it is not surprising that the first comment of nearly all who drove the car was that it now seemed too low-geared and fussy at speed.

The VX4/90 is a genuine 90 m.p.h. car, yet its engine begins to sound busy at about 60 m.p.h. in top, and although 85 m.p.h. can be held indefinitely with the rev. counter indicating 5,000 r.p.m., the mechanical roar and thrashing which goes with it is rather wearing. It seems a pity that the Laycock overdrive, offered by Vauxhall for the six-cylinder models, is still not available for the VX4/90 which would benefit from it even more. However, the noise level is consistent, and one can be surprised, when hurrying along a motorway, to glance down and see the rev. counter needle well into the red, and the unusually accurate speedometer indicating over 90 m.p.h.

Gearing

All of the indirect gears seem at first to be correspondingly low, but 70 m.p.h. is available in third if the rev counter needle is taken round to the start of the red sector, which extends from 5,400 to 6,000 r.p.m. Bottom gear takes the car up to only 29 m.p.h. and the initial take-off is rather slow. Even if the clutch is released viciously with lots of revs, the engine tends to die momentarily before pulling hard. Controlled clutch slip made a restart on 1 in 3 just possible, and also helps to give the best standing-start acceleration times.

The four-cylinder engine (with only three main bearings) is extremely responsive and free from any vibration periods, but there is a very harsh feel about it and the valve gear makes a lot of clattering noises. If the throttle is opened abruptly at low revs there is a bad flat-spot. Starting is always good, and the evidently rich carburation enabled cold starting without choke if a touch of throttle were given instead. The engine is quick to warm up, and pulls strongly at once after a night in the open. It has twin Zenith carburettors.

Vauxhalls are noted for light controls, and the mild pedal load needed to work the clutch is a relief in traffic. Also, the smoothness of take-up is such that there is no excuse for jerkiness. The floor-mounted gear change, optional on Victors, is standard with the VX4/90 and is pleasingly light and quick. The lever can be thrust from one gear to the next, up or down, without any need to double-declutch, and there is never any gear crash even during snatch changes. There is little resistance to movement and the driver does not have to stretch for the lever which has a revised shape. The characteristic gear whine, from which many could recognise the car as a Vauxhall even blindfold, is audible in the indirects.

An advantage of the reduction in wheel size is that the engine is even more tractable at low speeds, and although hardly practical in ordinary driving, acceleration from 10 m.p.h. in top gear is possible. There is also an unusually lively performance available in top gear, so that above 40 not a great deal is gained by changing down to third—the down-change to save the odd second or two is usually kept in reserve. The excellence of the gearchange may encourage one to use it, but this is not a car in which continual gearchanging is necessary for lively performance.

→

A forward-pivoted strut is fixed in place to hold the bonnet open. The distributor is obscured by heater pipes, but access to most other components is good, and all topping up can be done without having to burrow down into the engine compartment

MAKE: **Vauxhall**

TYPE: **VX4/90**

TEST CONDITIONS:
Weather   Sunny, cloudless sky with 10-15 m.p.h. wind
Temperature .. .. 18 deg. C (64 deg. F.)
Barometer .. .. .. 30·0in. Hg.
Surfaces .. .. Dry concrete and tarmac

WEIGHT
Kerb weight (with oil, water and half-full fuel tank): 20·4cwt (2,282lb-1,035kg)
Front-rear distribution, per cent .. F 52·8; R 47·2
Laden as tested .. 23·4cwt (2,618lb-1,187kg)

TURNING CIRCLES
Between kerbs .. L, 33ft 2in.; R, 34ft 4in.
Between walls .. L, 35ft 6in.; R, 36ft 3in.
Steering wheel turns lock to lock .. .. 4·3

PERFORMANCE DATA
Top gear m.p.h. per 1,000 r.p.m. .. .. 17·5
Mean piston speed at max. power .. 2,600ft/min
Engine revs. at mean max. speed .. 5,320 r.p.m.
B.h.p. per ton laden 73

OIL CONSUMPTION
Miles per pint SAE 20 600

FUEL CONSUMPTION
At constant speeds
30 m.p.h. 40·8 m.p.g.   70 m.p.h. 27·2 m.p.g.
40   ,,   40·4 ,,   80   ,,   22·4 ,,
50   ,,   36·7 ,,   90   ,,   18·7 ,,
60   ,,   32·0 ,,

Overall m.p.g. .. 23·3 (12·1 litres/100km)
Normal range m.p.g. 22-27 (12·8-10·5 litres/100km)
Test distance .. .. .. 1,068 miles
Estimated (DIN) m.p.g. 25·4 (11·1 litres/100km)
Grade .. .. .. Premium (96·2-98·6RM)

Speed range, gear ratios and time in seconds

m.p.h.	Top (3·9)	Third (5·3)	Second (8·3)	First (12·8)
10—30	10·4	7·4	4·7	—
20—40	10·3	6·6	4·8	—
30—50	10·7	7·5	—	—
40—60	11·7	9·1	—	—
50—70	13·9	11·0	—	—
60—80	20·2	—	—	—

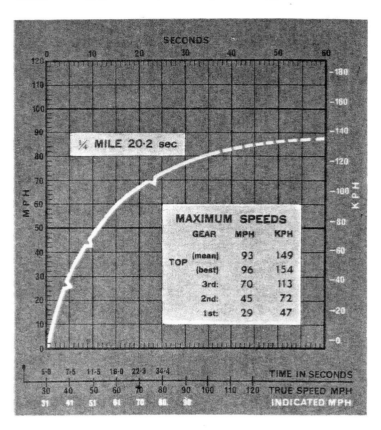

MAXIMUM SPEEDS

GEAR	MPH	KPH
TOP (mean)	93	149
TOP (best)	96	154
3rd:	70	113
2nd:	45	72
1st:	29	47

¼ MILE 20·2 sec

BRAKES	Pedal load	Retardation	Equiv. distance
(from 30 m.p.h. in neutral)	25lb	0·40g	75ft
	50lb	0·85g	35ft
	75lb	0·95g	31·7ft
Handbrake		0·40g	75ft

CLUTCH—Pedal load and travel—35lb and 5½in.

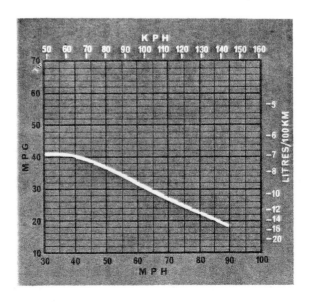

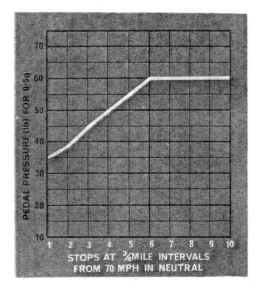

All doors have reasonably strong keeps. Thick and durable-looking carpet covers the floor, and the Ambla plastic upholstery is comfortable, but its dark brown colouring was liked less than the all-black of previous VX4/90s. Firm, deep crash padding on the facia offers accident protection

Vauxhall VX4/90 ...

Vauxhall recently added a limited-slip differential to the list of options for the VX4/90 (and for Victors), and this extra at £9 13s 4d was fitted on the test car. It gave the expected improvement in traction appreciated best when accelerating hard from rest in the rain, and it helps keep the car going on mud or soft ground. It also eliminates completely the earlier model's tendency to wheelspin and hop especially on changes in the road surface. Moreover, it also gives a marked improvement in the grip on corners in the wet, and the car can be accelerated hard through a bend on a slippery surface without tail slide. Adhesion is outstandingly good, and is owed equally to the sure-footed grip of the Avon radial-ply tyres which are offered without extra cost. Their drawback is considerable thump and vibration over poor surfaces—a small penalty for the greater security. On dry roads, the car can be cornered hard and with confidence. There is just the right amount of understeer, not enough to give any impression of nose-heaviness. A front anti-roll bar is fitted, but there is still a lot of body roll in hard cornering.

Strong counterbalance springs lift the boot lid as soon as the catch is released. Although not very deep, because of the fuel tank underneath, the compartment extends right forward and will prove large enough for most families

On both the washboard and the *pavé* sections of the M.I.R.A. test track there was such severe vibration, shake and noise that we abandoned the exercise and steered off very quickly; yet on all ordinary surfaces encountered in Britain, from fast main roads to poorly-surfaced secondaries, the car rides extremely well. Wheel reactions are firmly damped, and the suspension is soft enough to iron out irregularities with little jolt or bounce. On M1, the car absorbed very well the broken and deformed patchwork in the third lane, while on all surfaces there is—apart from the tyre thump mentioned—notable absence of road roar.

Excellent steering adds to the ease and confidence with which the car is handled at speed. It offers the all-too-rare combination of lightness and accuracy, and on one night of rain and lashing winds it took little correction to hold the car exactly on course. The lock also is good, and the combination of a 34ft turning circle with lightness helps greatly in manoeuvring. Not until the VX4/90 is offered up to a private garage is it realized that this is a deceptively big car, although one which can be parked easily.

Magnificent brakes were practically without equal on the previous model, and although on the 101 they are

Overriders with rubber inserts are available as extras. All doors can be locked without the key, by holding the exterior button down as the door is closed, and it is not necessary to use a key to open the boot unless it is locked

necessarily smaller, they do not lose much in efficiency. They are Girling discs at the front and self-wrapping drums at the rear, with a vacuum servo. They give the unusually high figure of 0·4g deceleration in response to a mere 25lb effort—a pedal load which, with many cars, barely gives enough response to record on the meter. Efficiency increases sharply as the pedal is pressed harder, but at the limit of 0·95g the car obviously needs better rear wheel adhesion and there is severe brake shudder. The point at which the rear wheels start to lock comes at only 50lb load on the pedal, and this excellent response to light loads is an important safety factor as well as reducing still more the effort of driving.

Our fade test brought a progressive increase in pedal load, until the stage where the brakes were smoking and tending to be rather rough; but recovery was quick. Fade is not sudden enough to surprise anyone in a long mountain descent, and it takes only a moment's respite to restore braking efficiency. The rear brakes are no longer self-adjusting. The handbrake is excellent, and holds on 1 in 3 with barely need for the lever to be pulled any harder than for normal parking.

VX4/90 ease of control is furthered by seats which provide good support and hold occupants in place on corners, and by very good visibility. The full width of the bonnet is in view from the driving seat, and its stainless steel edge strips are helpful markers when feeding the car through a narrow gap. Vauxhall have not obtained light steering by using a ridiculously large wheel—at 16in. dia. it feels just right, and is mounted at the correct angle to give a classic, comfortable driving position, with no need to peer over the top of the rim. The seats do not recline nor have they any backrest adjustment, but there is sufficient room both front and rear for tall people to sit comfortably. The seat upholstery is firmly sprung, does not accentuate suspension movements, and one emerges from the car after a long trip feeling relaxed and free from any aches or numbness.

A central lockable compartment provides sensibly large space for cameras and other possessions, and has its own key. All other locks on the car share the second key. Occasionally the lid failed to drop down in response to a touch on its release button. There are parcel shelves to either side, and map pockets on the front doors. Among further refinements included are a finger tip headlamp flasher, trip mileometer, and armrests on all doors, with ashtrays built into the rear ones. There is a sturdy grab handle for the passenger, but—perhaps as a safety measure—no vanity mirror behind the padded sun visor. The cigarette lighter costs £1 8s.

The new heater evolved for the 101 series certainly has terrific output, and the funnels to direct a proportion of the incoming air to the rear compartment are decidedly effective. Quite a torrent of air can be felt rushing past the front seat; but although the system is thermostatically controlled, we could not find any intermediate setting between hot and cold. The driver, in particular, finds also that his right foot gets cooked while the left one remains relatively cold.

TOTAL PRICE: £884 / £934 / £807 / £900 / £920

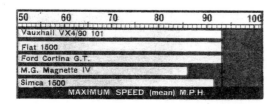

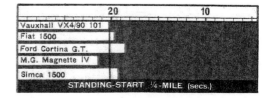

HOW THE VAUXHALL VX4/90 101 COMPARES:

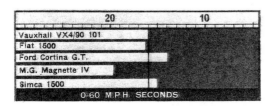

In wet weather caution is needed—the demister can fog the windscreen in an instant when switched on, before the matrix has had time to heat up. When either of the swivelling windows is opened at speed there is some shriek but it is not bad enough to deter one from leaving them open.

It would be too much to expect the same mechanical components in a slightly larger, heavier and fractionally faster car to give the same fuel economy as before; but in fact the overall consumption of 23.3 m.p.g. is under 2 m.p.g. lower than that of the previous VX4/90. This figure is fairly consistent in hard driving on ordinary roads and motorways, but with restraint it can be improved to 26 m.p.g. fairly easily. Ordinary premium fuel is satisfactory in spite of the 9.3 to 1 compression ratio. Up to 200 miles is the working range of the 10-gallon tank which, incidentally, has a slow filler prone to blow-back.

Wipers clear the screen very thoroughly by sweeping quite different overlapping arcs of about 90 deg on the driver's side, and nearly double this on the left. In the usual Vauxhall way, a triangular wiper knob helps one to pick the right control at night, and although two identical oval-shaped knobs are used for the driving and (optional) fog lamps, one soon remembers that the one pulls out and the other is turned, to switch on.

The big gains in this latest version of the sportsman's Vauxhall are extra room—especially in the boot, which is generously spacious—and the complete transformation in its roadholding. A number of other detail matters have been improved, but the car does now call for the greater refinement of a more advanced engine, and an overdrive or higher gearing.

SPECIFICATION : VAUXHALL VX4/90 101 FRONT ENGINE, REAR-WHEEL DRIVE

ENGINE

Cylinders	4-in-line
Cooling system	Water; pump, fan and thermostat
Bore	82mm (3.21in.)
Stroke	76mm (3.0in.)
Displacement	1,594 c.c. (97.4 cu. in.)
Valve gear	Overhead, pushrods and rockers
Compression ratio	9.3-to-1; option 7.0
Carburettors	2 Zenith
Fuel pump	AC mechanical
Oil filter	AC by-pass, renewable element
Max. power	73.8 b.h.p. (net) at 5,200 r.p.m.
Max. torque	98.7 lb ft (net) at 3,200 r.p.m.

TRANSMISSION

Clutch	Borg and Beck s.d.p., 8in. dia.
Gearbox	Four-speed, all-synchromesh, central remote-control change
Gear ratios	Top 1.0, Third, 1.36, Second 2.13, First 3.28, Reverse 3.05
Final drive	Hypoid, 3.9-to-1

CHASSIS and BODY

Construction	Integral with steel body

SUSPENSION

Front	Independent, coil springs and wishbones; anti-roll bar. Telescopic dampers
Rear	Live axle on semi-elliptic leaf springs; telescopic dampers

STEERING

Type	Recirculating ball
Wheel dia.	16in.

BRAKES

Make and type	Girling disc front, drum rear
Servo	Girling vacuum
Dimensions	F, 9in. dia.; R,9in. dia.; 1.75in. wide shoes
Swept area	F, 154 sq. in.; R, 99 sq. in. Total 253 sq. in. (216 sq. in. per ton laden)

WHEELS

Type	Pressed steel disc. 4in. wide rim
Tyres	Avon radial ply tubeless. Size 155—13in.

EQUIPMENT

Battery	12-volt 38-amp. hr.
Generator	Lucas 22 amp.
Headlamps	Lucas sealed filament 60/45-watt
Reversing lamp	Extra
Electric fuses	4 plus circuit breaker for lamps
Screen wipers	Single-speed, self-parking
Screen washer	Standard, Trico vacuum
Interior heater	Standard, fresh-air
Safety belts	Extra; ancorages provided
Interior trim	Ambla leathercloth seats, p.v.c. headlining
Floor covering	Woven pile carpet
Starting handle	No provision
Jack	Screw pillar
Jacking points	2 each side under sills
Other bodies	None

MAINTENANCE

Fuel tank	10 Imp. gallons (no reserve) (45.5 litres)
Cooling system	13.3 pints (including heater) (7.5 litres)
Engine sump	7.5 pints (4.3 litres) SAE20 or 20W. Change oil every 3,000 miles. Change filter element every 6,000 miles
Gearbox	2.4 pints SAE80. No change necessary
Final drive	2.5 pints SAE90. No change necessary
Grease	4 points every 30,000 miles
Tyre pressures	F, 24 p.s.i.; R, 27 p.s.i. (all conditions) radial ply tyres

Scale ⅛in to 1ft cushions uncompressed

velvet touch
vivid motoring

1.5 litres 4 cylinders. 81 b.h.p. at 5,200 r.p.m.
Twin carburettors. Special inlet manifold.
Aluminium cylinder head. Specially tuned
suspension for fast, tough driving.

Power-assisted brakes (discs in front).
4-speed all-synchro gears, floor-mounted lever.
Luxury for 4-5 adults. Comfort. Quiet.
Wide windows. Big boot. Heater. Screenclean.
Simple maintenance, just 4 greasing points.

Ask your dealer for a test run in the

VAUXHALL VX 4/90

£927. 15. 3 including purchase tax
Vauxhall Motors Ltd. Luton Beds.

Compare your car with the VX4/90

	VX4/90	YOUR CAR
Carburettors	2	
0-50 mph	11.9 secs	
top speed	90 +	
cylinder head	aluminium	
brakes	disc front	
servo assist	all brakes	
bhp	81 gr. @ 5200	
gears	4 all-synchro	
people in comfort	4 or 5	
boot	21.4 cu.ft.	
front seats	individual	
upholstery	'Ambla'	
heater	yes	
screenwash	yes	
rev-counter	yes	
doors	4	
seat belt anchors	yes	
padded fascia	yes	
underbody sealing	yes	
PRICE	£840.7.1 inc. tax	

Think hard about these comparisons. Odds are that either you can match the performance of the VX4/90 but not its comfort and capacity; or that you drive a saloon with nothing like the VX performance.

It's for people like you that Vauxhall build the VX4/90. It cannily combines saloon car space with vivid motoring — and the velvet touch.

Arrange a trial drive with your Vauxhall dealer.

VAUXHALL VX4/90